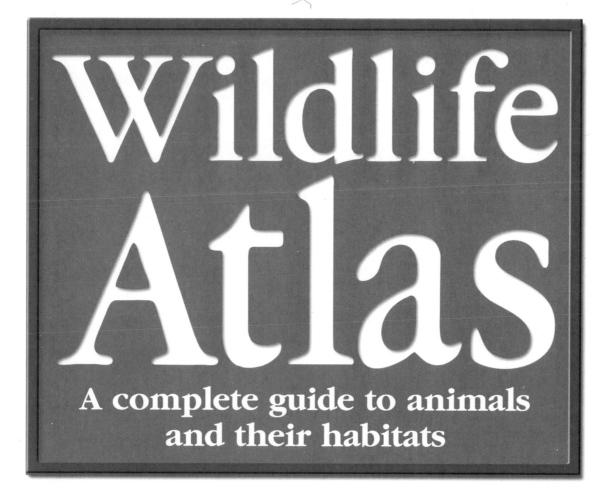

Wildlife Atlas

A complete guide to animals and their habitats

JOHN FARNDON

Reader's Digest

The Reader's Digest Association, Inc.
Pleasantville, New York • Montreal

A READER'S DIGEST BOOK

Copyright © 2002 Marshall Editions Developments Ltd
Text copyright © Barnsbury Books

BARNSBURY BOOKS
Based on an original concept from Barnsbury Books

A MARSHALL EDITION
Edited and designed by Marshall Editions Ltd
The Old Brewery, 6 Blundell Street, London N7 9BH, U.K.

Library of Congress Cataloging-in-Publication Data

Farndon, John
  Wildlife atlas : a complete guide to animals and their habitats / John Farndon.
     p.cm.
  Summary: Provides information about eight different habitats around the
  world and the various animals that live in each.
    ISBN 0-7621-0354-X
    1. Habitat (Ecology)--Juvenile literature. 2. Animal ecology--Juvenile
  literature. [1. Habitat (Ecology) 2. Animal ecology. 3. Ecology.] I. Title.

QH541.14 .F37 2002
591.7--dc21
                                                            2002017116

Address any comments about Wildlife Atlas to:
The Reader's Digest Association, Inc.
Trade Publishing
Reader's Digest Road, Pleasantville, NY 10570-7000

Originated in Italy by Articolor
Printed and bound in Portugal by Printer Portuguesa

10 9 8 7 6 5 4 3 2 1

Consultant Professor Bryan Turner

For Reader's Digest
Director, Trade Publishing Christopher T. Reggio
Executive Editor, Trade Publishing Dolores York
Editorial Director Christopher Cavanaugh
Senior Designer George McKeon
Senior Design Director Elizabeth Tunnicliffe
Contributing Copy Editor Vicki Fischer

For Barnsbury Books
Editorial and Research Angela Koo, John Farndon

For Marshall Editions
Designers Julia Harris, Rebecca Painter, Philip Letsu
Visualizer Ralph Pitchford
Managing Art Editor Helen Spencer
Art Director Simon Webb
DTP Manager Ali Marshall
Editors Nicola Munro, Elise See Tai
Managing Editors Julie Brooke, Clint Twist, Scarlett O'Hara
Publishing Director Linda Cole
Picture Researchers Su Alexander, Cynthia Frazer,
Sarah Stewart-Richardson
Production Anna Pauletti

Contents

INTRODUCTION

Perhaps uniquely in the universe, our planet teems with life. As human exploration penetrates to the darkest corners of the Earth, we are finding life in every nook and cranny, in every environment no matter how extreme. Strange fish lurk in the pitch black of the very deepest oceans. Birds are found nesting atop some of the world's highest mountains.

But what is most astounding, perhaps, is the sheer variety of life—swimming in the vast oceans, flying through the air, and slithering, crawling, or running over the world's land surfaces. More than 1.5 million species of animals have been named so far, and most zoologists believe there may be many, many more as yet undiscovered. There are over 4,000 known species of mammals, 6,800 species of reptiles, 4,780 amphibians, 9,000 species of birds, 24,000 fish, 1 million insects, and perhaps 400,000 other tiny creatures that go by the general name "invertebrates," including 60,000 kinds of spider.

We owe this rich diversity of life to hundreds of millions of years of evolution, hundreds of millions of years of subtle changes, generation by generation, as some creatures survived to pass on their quirks to their offspring and as others with their own quirks died out. Of course, those creatures best equipped for the prevailing conditions survived; those poorly equipped passed into the oblivion of extinction.

Conditions change, of course, and through time many, many creatures have gone the way of the dinosaurs—those mighty creatures once so well adapted they were lords of the Earth, but then rapidly finding themselves has-beens as the world changed around them. But conditions do not only vary through time; they vary across the face of the planet too.

Every region on Earth has its own unique conditions, and during the long roll of evolution, a unique range of creatures has developed to suit each particular place. An endless sequence of chance changes has created the host of different animal species that inhabit the Earth today, each particularly adapted to survive in its own special place, each occupying its own niche in the environment.

And just as every species has its home, so every home has its species. The gentle deciduous woodlands of Northeast America provide a habitat for a very different range of creatures, with its deer and badgers, from the wide open savanna of Africa with its lions and elephants. Climate, plant life, terrain, the availability of food and shelter, and many other factors have given every region its own distinctive range of creatures.

This book provides an overview of where the world's animals live and why they live there. The book travels the world, habitat by habitat, from the scorched grasslands of the tropics to the frozen wastes of the Arctic and Antarctic. Each chapter focuses on a particular habitat and introduces, continent by continent, the range of creatures that make this habitat their home—the predators, the grazing mammals, the birds of the air, the insects, the reptiles, and all the rest. Within each chapter special feature pages explore the nature of the habitat and the complex web of inter-relationships between all the animals that live there. Vivid wildlife panoramas peer into each habitat and capture a living moment in the Sumatran rain forest, the Siberian taiga, or South America's Gran Chaco.

Yet it is a sad fact that by the time you read this book, some of the animals in it may have vanished forever. Today we are witnessing what may be one of the greatest waves of animal extinctions ever, as more and more species fall victim to rampaging human activity. There are now over 5,000 species in the high risk category, and many more under threat.

Experts predict that a fifth of all the world's animal species may be lost in the next 20 years.

Many factors are to blame for this impending tragedy. The loss of habitats as forest is cleared by farmers and loggers. The relentless spread of cities. The poisoning of the land by pollutants and pesticides. The deadly gun of the hunter. The more we know and understand the reasons for this massacre, the better equipped we will be to prevent it—so this book identifies some of the key species that are in danger in each habitat and the factors that are putting their existence at risk.

Despite this, the world is still blessed by an astonishing wealth of wildlife, and it is this that the *Wildlife Atlas* celebrates in presenting a unique view of the animal and plant life of our planet.

JOHN FARNDON

Animal homes

There are many ways of dividing the world into natural regions. Zoologists divide it into five regions. Climatologists divide it by climate. Botanists divide it by plant type. There is a close relationship between climate and vegetation type,

Grassland food web

and both play a key role in determining where each kind of animal lives. So in this book, the world is divided into broad "habitats"—regions where a particular environment for animals is created by the climate and plant life—such as tropical rain forests and deserts.

Sumatran rain forest

Animal groups

The animal world is divided into animals that have backbones, called vertebrates, and those that have none, called invertebrates. Invertebrates are mostly small creatures, such as insects and mollusks—although giant squids grow up to 60 ft (about 18 m) long. The main groups of vertebrates are: fish, birds, amphibians, reptiles, and mammals. In this book, birds and mammals are further grouped according to where they spend most of their time (birds of the air and ground birds) or how they find their food (birds of prey, predatory mammals, browsers, foragers, and grazing mammals). The groups vary from habitat to habitat, because some kinds of creatures are rare or absent, while others are much more common.

Tropical grasslands

More than one-third of the world's land surface is covered in grass. Much of the grassland was created by farmers who cleared forests for their livestock to graze on. But there is still a great deal of grassland that is entirely natural, especially in the tropics.

•

Grasslands occur in the tropics wherever, for at least half the year, there is not enough rain for trees to grow. Apart from a few isolated thorn and palm trees, grass here stretches as far as the eye can see under wide-open skies. In the wet season, the grass is green and lush. But in the dry season, the land is parched and the grass turns yellow.

•

Even so, grasslands are incredibly productive habitats. Every square yard (0.8 sq m) of African grassland grows over four pounds (1.8 kg) of plant matter a year—half as much as pine forest produces—from just a thin covering of grass. So tropical grasslands can support a huge amount of wildlife and are home to some of the world's most spectacular creatures.

Where are tropical grasslands?

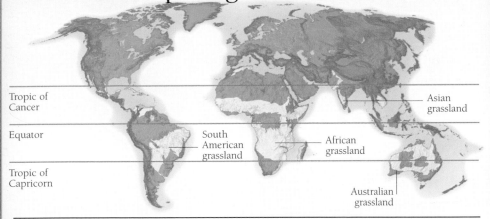

Tropic of Cancer

Equator

Tropic of Capricorn

South American grassland

African grassland

Asian grassland

Australian grassland

Comparing tropical grasslands

Over 160 species of grass including bunch grass and *Briza*

Herbaceous palm

Quebracho thorn tree

Acacia thorn

Elephant grass up to 10 ft (3 m) tall

Euphorbia tree

Baobab tree with thick trunk for water storage

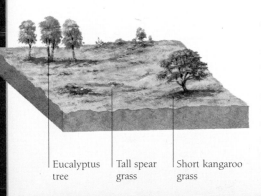

Eucalyptus tree

Tall spear grass

Short kangaroo grass

South America

South American grasslands are often parklike landscapes of clustered trees and shrubs dotted with tall palm trees. Here and there is espinal, a dry forest of spiny, thorny shrubs and low trees. The thorny quebracho tree shoots up almost everywhere in the South American grasslands and in places forms dense thickets that rise like islands amid the sea of grasses. There are over 160 species of grass, some growing as high as a person on horseback.

Africa

The savanna is the tropical grassland covering much of central Africa, especially in the east. The savanna varies with the length of the dry season. Stretching along the dry southern edge of the Sahara Desert is the Sahel—a vast area of thorn savanna that is dry, sparse grassland scattered with thin trees. Dry thorny grassland also covers a large area of southern Africa at the fringes of the Kalahari Desert. There are places that are relatively moist, where small forests of broad-leaved trees, such as euphorbias, grow quite densely.

Australia

In Australia, the tropical grass of the bush covers a huge arc round the north of the continent from east to west. In the northeast, in Queensland, the grass is distinctive; in the moister areas tall spear grass and shorter kangaroo grass grow. Most Australian grassland trees are evergreens, such as eucalyptus, acacia, and bauhinia. Their waxy leaves reduce water loss, which helps them to survive the dry season. In the northwest, the most common trees are baobabs.

Tropical grassland environments

Tropical grasslands are warm—typically averaging over 80°F (27°C) during the day. In the dry season temperatures can soar to 130°F (54°C). Most get 20–60 in (500–1,500 mm) of rain a year, but most of this comes in a five- to eight-month wet season. The rest of the year is almost bone-dry. Even in the wet season, water evaporates quickly in the warm air.

°C | °F | Temperature | Rainfall | mm | in

J F M A M J J A S O N D

Sun and rain

This graph shows rainfall month by month, and the average monthly temperature for Nairobi in the African savanna. The wettest months are from November to May. The dry season begins in June and also lasts five months, until the rains come again in November.

Thunderstorms

When it does rain on tropical grasslands, it rains in torrents. Typically, huge gray thunderclouds build up in the heat of the morning, then the storm begins in mid-afternoon. Isolated trees are often struck by lightning, starting fires in the dry grass.

New grass

In the hot dry season, the grass can turn to straw and may even be burned away by bush fires. It looks dead, but even though the grass is burned, its roots are safe under the soil. The grass soon sprouts new shoots when the rains finally come.

South American tropical grasslands

The tropical grasslands of South America are very different from those of Africa. African savannas are huge expanses of grass, where vast herds of large grazing animals can thrive. But South America's grasslands are much more varied, with bogs and dense scrub in many places. So, instead of grazers, the dominant animals are large rodents, such as capybaras and agoutis, and foragers, such as tapirs and peccaries, as well as many birds.

The greater rhea

Greater rheas are huge birds that cannot fly, but can run very fast. Although rhea numbers have been severely reduced by hunting and farming, they can still be seen in groups of about 30. At breeding time, the male mates with several females. He then makes a shallow nest on the ground and incubates the eggs of all his females.

Ground birds

The scarcity of trees means that many species of bird of the South American grasslands are ground-dwellers. Besides the rhea, tinamous, nothura, rhynchotus, quails, and others strut through the grass, and various finches forage for seeds.

The Gran Chaco is a vast, dry lowland plain covering 280,000 sq miles (725,000 sq km) of central South America between the Andes and the Paraguay and Paraná rivers.

Capybara

Capybaras are the largest of all living rodents, growing to 4 ft (1.25 m) long and weighing over 120 lb (55 kg). They are quite shy and live in groups along riverbanks—diving in quickly if predators, such as jaguars, appear. They browse on leaves, but, in farming areas, they may occasionally steal melons and grain.

Rodents

The grassland swamps are a good habitat for large rodents. Besides the capybara, agoutis, and coatis, various cavies and taco-taco scrabble through the reeds. Many small rodents live here, too, such as alcodons and various mice. There is also a giant otter, which is much bigger than European otters.

King vulture

King vultures have wings spanning nearly 6 ft (1.8 m). They feed mostly on carrion—animals that are already dead. They are strong fliers, spending hours soaring high up, scanning the ground for corpses. Vultures have sharp eyes and a good sense of smell, too, which is unusual for birds.

Reptiles and amphibians

Swamps and rivers provide ample habitats for many reptiles and amphibians. Besides snakes, such as boas and pit vipers, there are other reptiles, such as crocodile-like caimans, river turtles, iguanas, and lizards, such as the teyou. Poisonous tree frogs and toads, such as *Bufo rufus*, are often seen here.

Boa constrictor

Boas are a family of large constrictor snakes that kill their prey by squeezing it. They swallow their victims whole, then spend days digesting them. Special jaws allow their mouths to open very wide. A large meal, such as a capybara, can be seen as a lump moving gradually down the snake's body as it is digested.

Birds of prey

The birds and small creatures of the South American grasslands make rich pickings for a host of predatory birds, such as hawk-eagles, Swainson's hawk, chimango, caracara, falcons, chacalacas, kites, and nighthawks. Black vultures and king vultures swoop down on carrion.

The Llanos is a vast area of low-lying grass and swampland covering 350,000 sq miles (900,000 sq km) of Venezuela and northeast Colombia.

The Gran Sabana is a high tableland of grass and scrub, bounded by steep cliffs. Its inaccessibility makes it a valuable refuge for many rare species.

ATLANTIC OCEAN

Paraná

The Cerrado is a land of grasses and shrubs south of the Amazon rain forest, covering one quarter of Brazil. It is as big as western Europe and home to five percent of all the world's animal species.

Puma

Also known as mountain lion and cougar, the puma is a graceful cat that roams throughout the Americas. Adults grow up to 10 ft (3 m) long and weigh up to 220 lb (100 kg). Despite its size, it has a voice like a domestic cat, only louder. It is a hunter and feeds on deer and guanaco.

Predatory mammals
Four big cats prowl the grasslands—jaguars, jaguarundis, ocelots, and pumas, plus smaller cats like the gato pajero and gato montes. Two large dogs also hunt here: the rare maned wolf and the rarer bush dog.

Rufous-tailed jacamar

This colorful bird perches on branches, waving its head as it scans the air for insects. When it spots one, it darts off to snap it up in midair, then flies back to its perch. It may bang the insect against the branch to kill it before eating it. The birds lay two to four eggs in a tunnel in the ground, which is dug by the female.

Fish
The rivers and swamps of the South American grasslands hold more species of fish than any comparable habitat. There are characins, such as the dorado, the pencil fish, voracious meat-eating piranhas, and their harmless cousins, the pacus.

Grazing mammals
The grasslands support few large grazing animals except llamalike guanaco and deer, such as pampas deer, and gray and little brockets. Herds of these animals have been much reduced as cattle ranches have spread.

Red piranha

Piranhas are barely 15 in (38 cm) long, but they swim together in such huge shoals that they can strip a large animal to its skeleton in just a few minutes with their razor-sharp teeth. Usually, they are attracted to prey by the scent of blood.

Pampas deer

This tiny deer once roamed down into the pampas (treeless plains) of Argentina. Now farming and hunting have wiped it out from much of its range and it lives only in the Cerrado and the Gran Chaco.

Birds of the air
Many of the birds seen in the air above the South American grasslands are seasonal migrants, such as swifts, orioles, and wrens. Natives include anhingas, woodpeckers, parakeets, hyacinthine and other macaws, doves, and flycatchers. Insect-eaters include ovenbirds, puffbirds, hummingbirds, and tanagers.

Insects
The South American grasslands are home to a huge range of insects, including many flies and beetles and beautiful swallowtail butterflies. However, the dominant species are termites and ants, especially fire ants and army ants.

Giant armadillo

Giant armadillos are stout, short-legged animals that grow up to 40 in (1 m) long. Unusually for grassland animals, they move slowly, but they are protected by a tough armor of horny plates. When attacked they scurry to their burrow or simply curl up. They feed mainly on termites, digging into their nests with strong, curved front claws.

Army ant

Over 150 species of army ant live in tropical South America. They get their name because they march in troops to find prey. Unlike other ants, they do not build nests, but live together in "bivouacs." These can contain a million or more ants.

Foraging mammals
Among the foragers are piglike animals, such as the peccary and tapir. Both are related to horses. Ants and termites are so abundant that they provide food for quite large animals, such as the giant anteater and the giant and nine-banded armadillos. Porcupines feed on plant stems and fruit.

9

Survival in grasslands

For the animals of the South American grasslands, life is a constant battle for survival. The long months of the dry season mean that every creature has to struggle to find food and water, while the lack of hiding places among trees makes life dangerous all year round. For plant-eating animals, survival means eating grass or the roots and tiny fruit of scrubby trees. But these herbivores provide food for a range of large predators, such as jaguars, pumas, and maned wolves.

Who eats what

As in every environment, animals in the South American grasslands depend on each other for survival. Plant-eaters get the food they need from surrounding vegetation. But all other animals need to eat other animals to survive. Jaguars eat animals like rhea and deer, while wolves eat armadillos, and armadillos eat termites. Indeed, all grassland animals are linked together in chains of food dependence, and these food chains are interwoven in a complex, finely balanced web of dependence. A change to even one tiny part of this web—perhaps due to human intervention—can upset the whole balance.

Caracaras often feed on carrion early in the morning. But they also swoop down on small birds like ovenbirds and puffbirds.

Flies play a vital part in the grassland ecology, spreading pollen as they feed on plants, and clearing waste as they feed on dung and dead creatures.

Agoutis are too small to cope with the tall grass, so live in the shorter grass where they scrabble for fallen fruit. Their hearing is so acute that they can find the fruit by listening for the quiet thud as it falls.

Giant armadillos are tough, armored creatures with incredibly powerful front claws. They use these to dig out termites' nests to get at the termites, which they eat.

Termites eat the wood of rotting trees and roots. Their activity helps in the breakdown of vegetation to soil.

Termite

Earthworms play a vital role in processing the soil and making it fertile. The soil goes in one end, passes through their gut and emerges from the other end.

The South American caecilian is a blind, burrowing amphibian related to lizards. It lives in the soil and feeds on earthworms.

Grassland adaptations: Long legs

With nowhere to hide, many creatures rely on speed to escape predators. Indeed, many grassland animals are among the world's fastest runners. Thomson's gazelles in Africa reach 50 mph (80 km/h). The rhea's African cousin, the ostrich, can tear along at 40 mph (65 km/h). To achieve these speeds, grazing animals like gray brockets and rheas have developed long, slender legs. Some predators, such as cheetahs, can run just as fast to catch them.

Gray brocket

Muscles are high on the legs and linked to the lower legs only by tendons to keep the lower legs light.

The leg bones are very long.

The ankle rotates a long way for maximum thrust.

Unlike other mammals, gray brockets have just two toes and run on the tips for maximum speed.

Rhea

The ankle and foot bones have fused into the lower leg for maximum length.

The rhea's toes have grown enormously long to propel it at high speed.

Puffbirds sally out from perches on branches to catch large insects in flight. Sometimes, they drop to the ground to forage for ants.

Maned wolves prey on armadillos and agoutis, as well as cuis (wild guinea pigs), rabbits, and viscachas (burrowing rodents). They also eat insects and birds as well as fruit and sugarcane.

Ovenbirds are small warblers that forage on the ground, poking through the grass and scrub for ants, termites, and spiders.

Gray brockets are small deer that live only in tall grass where they can hide. They feed on the tops of grass stalks and fruit from caesalpina and zizyphur trees.

Greater rheas live in the tall grass and feed on the grass tops—often feeding with deer herds. They also eat fruit and insects.

Jaguars prey on the larger grassland animals—brockets, rheas, and capybaras. They also attack peccaries, but the peccaries can often fight them off.

Capybaras feed on the short grasses by the waterside, and so avoid competing with deer (and farmers' cattle).

Jaguar

The jaguar has a bulky build, but, like many predators, in grass it is very quick and graceful. It can reach high speeds over short distances, climb trees, and even swim well. It relies on getting in close to its prey unnoticed, or lying silently in wait to make a kill. When it catches prey, its strong jaws can pulverize skulls.

Wildlife at risk!

Maned wolf
Fewer than 2,200 maned wolves now survive—mainly because their natural habitat has been destroyed as Bolivian and Paraguayan ranchers convert grassland to soybean farms. Many have been shot, too, by farmers angered by the wolves' fondness for chickens.

Guanaco
Guanacos are South America's largest land mammal, but their population has fallen dramatically. A century ago, there were over 8 million guanaco. Now there are only about 100,000—and numbers are dwindling fast as ranchers fence off grazing land and sheep compete for grass.

The human factor
Huge areas of grassland have been taken over for livestock farming in recent years, especially in the Brazilian Cerrado, but the impact on wildlife has received little attention. Putting cows and sheep to graze and erecting fences is less dramatic than clearing rain forest, but its effect on wildlife can be just as devastating.

The Gran Chaco

Stretching from the foothills of the Andes in the west to the turbulent waters of the Paraná River in the east, the Gran Chaco is a rolling plain, covering 280,000 sq miles (725,000 sq km). It lies at the heart of South America in Paraguay and Argentina, and its name comes from the Quechua Indian word for hunting land because of its abundance of animals. Much of it is a sea of grass, often growing as tall as a rider on horseback. Here and there, mounds topped by dense thickets of quebracho trees rise like dark green islands. In the scorching dry season, temperatures can soar to 116°F (47°C) and the grass turns to straw. In May, however, the rains come and grass roots that have survived hidden under the soil send out new shoots.

Afternoon on the Chaco

The dry season is upon the Chaco, and thundering rainstorms from the Amazon to the north evaporate into vast, china-blue skies. This is the time when the grass begins to hum with life. Millions of migratory birds—orioles, puffbirds, siskins—flock in from the north to feast on the fruit that the ancient trees bring forth year after year.

•

Down by the water hole, still full from the rains, a jaguar sits quite still in the grasses watching an unwary capybara. A green tree boa slithers around a tree, eyeing up the puffbird sitting on a branch, while a poisonous waxy leaf frog looks down into the water.

•

Nearby, tapirs scurry through the long grass. A long-limbed maned wolf lies quietly, waiting for the night to fall so it can go hunting. Farther away, wading sedately through the grass, are a pair of great rheas, the biggest birds in South America.

•

Everywhere, the plain is studded with mounds built by termites for their nests. Listen, and you can just pick up the scratch, scratch, snuffle as an anteater breaks its way in, to get at the scurrying termites. Far away, you can hear faintly on the breeze two guanacos making a strange, throaty sound called "gobbling" in greeting, while nearby the rest of the herd grazes quietly.

KEY

1 Waxy leaf frog	9 Maned wolf
2 Agouti	10 Red cardinal
3 Dorado	11 Rhea
4 Piranha	12 Tapir
5 Capybara	13 Giant armadillo
6 Emerald boa	14 Guanaco
7 Jaguar	15 Gray brocket
8 Giant anteater	16 Blue morpho

African grasslands

The vast savanna grasslands of Africa are among the most spectacular of all wildlife habitats, home to some of the world's largest mammals. Everywhere, there are herds of large grazing animals, such as antelopes and zebras. There are browsers, too, such as elephants and rhinos. Then there are large predators—most famously the big cats, such as lions and cheetahs.

Sahel
The Sahel is where the dry northern bushlands or "Sudan" savanna merge into the Sahara. Rare oryx, damas, dorcas, and red-fronted gazelles live here.

Browsers and foragers
Savanna trees provide food for browsers, such as elephants, giraffes, black and white rhinos, warthogs, and various antelopes—eland, kudu, gerenuk, steenbok, and Kirk's dik-dik. Yet, as more savanna is used for farming, trees are becoming less abundant as a food source.

African elephant
African elephants are the largest land animals. Bulls (adult males) stand 11 ft (3.4 m) high and weigh more than 5 tons. Elephants eat for 16 hours a day, feeding mainly on leaves, and often knock down trees to get at high branches. They also dig up roots and shrubs with their tusks. Family groups of females and young are led by the oldest female. Adult males roam alone.

Bushveld
In the south, the dry savanna fringes are called bushveld. Large herds of tsessebe, kudu, springbok, and hartebeest live here, as well as small groups of dik-dik.

Impala
Impala are among the most graceful antelopes, known for their agile running and jumping. To escape predators, such as lions and hunting dogs, they can travel 33 ft (10 m) in a single leap and race along at 50 mph (80 km/h). The strongest males lead herds of females and young.

Primates
Baboons and vervet monkeys sleep in trees to avoid predators, and vervet monkeys often forage in the trees, too. Greater and lesser bush babies spend their lives entirely in the trees and leap agilely from branch to branch.

Birds of prey
Many birds of prey find rich pickings here, including bateleur snake eagles, gabar goshawks, augur buzzards, marabou storks, and vultures, such as Ruppell's Griffon. These feed on the carcasses of large animals killed by lions and dogs.

Olive baboon
Baboons are big monkeys with strong jaws. They live on the ground in troops, which contain females and males of all ages. There is a strict hierarchy, but they do form friendships with one another.

Grazing mammals
Savanna grasses provide food for huge herds of grazers—zebras, waterbucks, and buffaloes; many antelope species, including sables and roans; wildebeests and hartebeests; and many kinds of gazelles, such as Thomson's and Grant's.

Secretary bird
Secretary birds are nearly 6 ft (1.8 m) tall. They get their name from their long head feathers, which look like the quill pens clerks once stuck behind their ears. They are famed for their ability to pin down and kill snakes with their feet.

Reptiles and amphibians

The lack of moisture means few amphibians live in the savanna, but there are many reptiles, including numerous chameleons, such as Jackson's and Meller's, barking geckos, lizards, leopard tortoises, and snakes.

Nile

Lake Victoria

Boomslang snake

The boomslang snake lies in wait on tree branches for chameleons and birds, with its front end hanging motionless in the air. If provoked, it will inflate its neck, then strike. Although less than 2 ft (60 cm) long, it is very dangerous to humans, with a poisonous bite that causes internal bleeding and death.

Serengeti

East Africa is the heartland of the grass savanna. The Serengeti in Tanzania is home to over half a million buffaloes, wildebeests, zebras, and gazelles, as well as elephants, giraffes, rhinos, lions, and cheetahs, plus 450 species of birds.

Insects

Under the savanna are vast nests of harvester termites that send out workers to forage for grass to feed the young. Flesh flies and carrion beetles feed on rotting carcasses left by vultures. Occasionally, vast swarms of locusts appear and may devastate crops.

Praying mantis

Praying mantises get their name because they hold their front legs together as if praying. They are the most fearsome predators of the insect world. They can even seize and eat small frogs. Typically, they make a kill with a swift bite to the neck. Female mantises will often bite the male's head off while mating.

Rock hyrax

On rock outcrops in the savanna live rabbit-sized creatures called hyraxes. They look like guinea pigs, but are related to elephants. In fact, the hyrax has a brain like an elephant's, a stomach like a horse's, and a skeleton like a rhino's.

Ground birds

With scant cover in the open savanna, there are fewer ground birds here than in some habitats. The flightless ostrich relies on running fast on its long legs to escape from predators. Other ground birds include yellow-billed and ground hornbills, kori bustards, and helmeted guinea fowls.

Small mammals

The savanna is famed for its large animals, but many small mammals scurry among the grasses, including elephant shrews, striped mice, and spring hares. Zorillas are skunklike mammals that hunt at night and rest in burrows by day. Like skunks, they spray an odor when alarmed.

Predatory mammals

The herds of hoofed grazers provide prey for big cats, such as lions, cheetahs, and leopards, and for dogs, such as hyenas and jackals. Cheetahs use speed to catch prey, such as gazelles, while hyenas and lions rely on teamwork.

Lion

Lions are among the biggest of the big cats. Males, with their great manes, are 10 ft (3 m) long and weigh up to 500 lb (230 kg), but the females do most of the hunting. Lions live in families called prides and usually eat every four days or so, consuming up to 110 lb (50 kg) of meat in a meal. They spend around 20 hours a day resting.

Oxpecker

Oxpeckers ride around on the backs of cattle, zebras, and rhinos, where they feed on ticks, helping to keep these animals free of parasites. One oxpecker can eat 2,000 ticks in a day. Oxpeckers hiss when alarmed, warning their hosts of danger.

Birds of the air

The savanna air is filled with birds, such as "go-away" birds (turacos), shrikes, flycatchers, starlings, hoopoes, rollers, bee-eaters, and many weaver birds, including vast flocks of quelea.

Sociable weaver bird

Sociable weavers get their name because they live together in unique nest colonies built of grass and mud in trees. With thatchlike roofs, the nests are up to 13 ft (4 m) high and 26 ft (8 m) long. Inside, there are up to 300 chambers, each home to a pair of birds. The chambers are set in clusters, each with its own entrance tunnel in the "basement." A few birds work all year-round to keep the nest tidy.

Grazers and browsers

The alternating wet and dry seasons in East Africa's Serengeti create the world's most amazing animal migrations. Every May, the rains stop, the land dries up, and vast herds of wildebeests begin to move in search of grass and water—snorting, bucking, and kicking up dust. They are joined in their trek by a multitude of zebras and antelopes—and are tailed by hungry lions and dogs. When the rains come again and fresh grass springs up, the herds return to complete a yearly migration cycle, during which they cover more than 1,500 miles (2,400 km).

Grassland adaptations: Browsing levels

Just as each grazer has adapted to make the most of certain grass conditions, so each browsing animal in the savanna has adapted to reach branches at different heights. Many browsers, such as rhinos and dik-diks, can reach lower branches, so competition here is severe; but big animals, such as elephants and giraffes, can reach much higher.

The giraffe uses its tongue to twist off leaves and twigs from branches 16 ft (4.9 m) up.

With its trunk, an elephant can pull down branches almost as high.

Gerenuks stand on their hind legs to reach high branches.

Elands use their horns to twist off shoulder-high branches.

WET SEASON

1. In the wet season, when the grass is plentiful, herds of zebras, wildebeests, and Thomson's gazelles intermingle on the high southeastern plains. Calves and foals are born in February.

7. Toward the end of October, the skies darken, the rains begin to fall, and the herds begin their journey back to the grassy plains of the southeast.

6. As the drought takes its toll, Griffon vultures that have been trailing the herds swoop down on animals that have died.

The great migration

The great wildebeest migration in the Serengeti has developed over tens of thousands of years, and is minutely attuned to variations in the environment. The herds rarely move at exactly the same time, or along the same route, and the migration changes in response to local variations in grass growth. In some years, a dry spell may set the herds moving from the open plains earlier; fire damage may block the path in others—then attract the animals the following year as fresh growth springs up. The timing of the rut, too, seems to vary to coincide with a full moon.

SE

NW

2. Toward the end of the wet season, the herds begin to gather for their migration and males start their ritual mating fights or ruts.

Thomson's gazelles trail behind the wildebeests feeding on the high-protein seeds and young shoots left behind after the wildebeests have eaten down the leafy grass stalks.

3. By the time the trek begins, zebra herds are 200,000 strong, Thomson's gazelle herds are half a million strong, and wildebeests a million and a half strong.

Wildebeests follow the zebras and feed on the lower leafy part of the grass left behind after the zebras have eaten.

Zebras lead the way, eating the coarse top layer of red oat grass. As they push on through the tall grass, they make a path for the small animals to follow.

D R Y   S E A S O N

4. As the dry season progresses, the herds move on farther to the northwest into more wooded areas. Many die as they cross crocodile-infested rivers.

5. Toward the end of the dry season, rivers dry up and water holes shrink. The herds, led by zebras, reach the woodlands of the northwest.

Wildlife at risk!

White rhinoceros
Next to elephants, white rhinos are the largest land animals. In Asia, their horn is thought to be an aphrodisiac, so rhinos are killed illegally for their horns. There are now barely 7,000 left. Gamekeepers cut off the rhino's horns to save them from being killed, but they regrow.

Grevy's zebra
Grevy's is the largest zebra and lives in arid parts of the savanna. In the 1970s, the species was decimated by poaching, because the skins were fashionable. Now the zebras are protected from poachers, but are threatened instead by growing cattle herds taking grazing land.

The growing desert
A drier climate in recent times has reduced the savanna fringes to desert. The problem has been made much worse as remaining areas are overgrazed, both by herds squeezed into a smaller area, and by farmers' livestock.

Hunting cheetah
The cheetah is the world's greatest sprinter. Because cover is sparse on the savanna, a cheetah relies on an explosive burst of speed to catch prey, such as a gazelle, and can reach 60 mph (100 km/h) in just five seconds. It leaves the ground twice in its running cycle—first with front and hind legs bunched up (pictured), then with them fully extended. During one of these leaps, the cheetah can travel almost 23 ft (7 m) through the air.

Australian grasslands

The vast, scrubby, rolling plains and plateaus of Australia's empty interior, or outback, are home to many of the continent's unique range of creatures, from kangaroos and wallabies to bandicoots and marsupial moles. Much of the outback is very arid, and creatures that live here must cope with little water. In lusher areas, wild animals have to compete with sheep and other livestock.

Red kangaroo

Red kangaroos are the biggest kangaroos—the biggest of all marsupials, standing over 6 ft (1.8 m) tall. They can travel at 40 mph (65 km/h) and leap 30 ft (9 m) in a single bound. They get their name from the male's back and chest, which turns red in the breeding season. Females are called "blue fliers" because of their blue-gray fur.

Grazing mammals

Australia has no native hoofed grazers. Instead, it has the kangaroo family with their strong back legs and long feet for hopping. There are 69 species, divided into two families—macropods (kangaroos and wallabies) and the smaller potoroids (potoroos and bettongs).

Wedge-tailed eagle

These eagles are Australia's biggest birds of prey, with 7½ ft- (2.3 m-) wingspans. In groups they can kill a kangaroo. The Tasmanian species is now endangered.

Birds of prey

Since big birds of prey can reach Australia, it has many species that are also found elsewhere, such as black kites. But there are local varieties, such as the Australian kestrel, the gray goshawk, and Australian hobby.

Insects and spiders

Australia's grasslands are home to many ants and termites, including the magnetic termite which aligns its nest north-south. There are many cicadas, beetles, flies, and spiders, too.

Giant stick insect

Australia has many species of giant stick insect. In 2001, a species thought long extinct was found living on an island off the east coast. It is 6 in (15 cm) long and is said to look like a walking sausage.

The Great Western Plateau
Covering most of western Australia, the Great Western Plateau is vast. It is 1,000–1,500 ft (300–460 m) high and is mostly covered in mulga and mallee scrub.

GULF OF CARPENTARIA

GIBSON DESERT

GREAT VICTORIA DESERT

GREAT AUSTRALIAN BIGHT

Ground birds

With few large predators, ground birds have flourished. Besides the emu, there are ground parrots like the turquoise grass parrot, as well as bowerbirds and "megapods"—large birds, such as mallee fowl and brush-turkey, which lay their eggs in mounds.

Emu

The emu is the world's second largest living bird, growing 6 ft (1.8 m) tall. It has only stubby wings and cannot fly, but can run on its long legs at speeds of up to 30 mph (50 km/h). If cornered, it kicks hard. It feeds mainly on roots, fruits, and leaves.

Frilled lizard

When frightened, the frilled lizard may lie camouflaged like a stick. When spotted, it opens its mouth wide, flings open its frilled ruff, and hisses loudly. However, it is actually quite harmless. It lives mainly in trees, but it also runs on the ground, and can travel up to 30 ft (9 m) in a single leap.

Reptiles and amphibians
In the Australian grasslands lurk many highly venomous snakes of the elapid family, including the deadly brown snake and the taipan. Australia also has about 500 species of lizard, including the gecko, skink, and giant goanna. In the northern rivers, there are smaller cousins of the giant estuarine crocodiles of the coast.

Fish
Australia's interior is dry, but its rivers and billabongs are teeming with fish, including the huge Murray cod, mouth almighties, yellowbellies, boomer bass, rainbowfish, and gudgeons. Little smelts and yabbies (crayfish) are found in hot, muddy pools.

Barramundi

The barramundi is a huge fish, up to 6 ft (1.8 m) long. It spawns in rivers and lakes in northern Australia before swimming to the sea. It starts life as a male and remains so until it reaches the sea. Then after five years, it becomes female to swim back up river to spawn. It is thought the salt water of the sea stimulates the sex change.

Small mammals
The Australian grasslands are home to many small mammals, including small marsupials unique to Australia, such as the marsupial mouse, bandicoot, wombat, and the mouselike phascogale. Many aestivate (stay dormant) in summer to cope with the heat.

Egg-laying mammals
Australia's long isolation has allowed two unique primitive egg-laying mammals, or "monotremes," to survive—the platypus and echidna.

Echidna

Echidnas, or spiny anteaters, are egg-laying mammals measuring about 20 in (50 cm) long. There are two species, each with short legs and strong claws for digging into the ground to get at ants, a long thin snout, and a long tongue for licking up the ants.

Predatory mammals
Before dingos arrived with seafarers 3,000 years ago, Australia's only large predator was the thylacine, a wolflike marsupial. Dingos drove thylacines to extinction on mainland Australia and are now the only large predators.

Budgerigar

Now kept in cages in homes all around the world, the budgerigar is a parakeet (small parrot) native to the Australian grasslands. Wild budgies are always green and travel in large flocks. They rarely stay in one place for long, moving on constantly in search of food. They feed on seeds, mainly in the morning to avoid the hottest part of the day.

Birds of the air
The Australian grasslands' rich bird life includes many parakeets and cockatoos, best known of which is the colorful galah, known for its raucous call. There are also many nectar-sipping honey-eaters and insect-eating bee-eaters.

Dingo

The dingo is a wild form of the domestic dog thought to have originated in Asia. Before the Europeans arrived, dingos' main prey was kangaroos and wallabies. Nowadays, they also hunt rabbits and sheep, so farmers try to fence them out and poison them.

Hairy-nosed wombat

The rare hairy-nosed, or plains, wombat is one of the world's largest burrowing animals, up to 3½ ft (1.1 m) long. With its shovel-like front paws, it can dig long burrows where it rests in the day. Like other marsupials, it carries its young in a pouch until they are big enough to survive outside.

Pouched mammals

One hundred million years ago, Australia began to drift away from the rest of the world's continents, and a unique range of wildlife developed there in isolation. In particular, there are two kinds of mammal found almost nowhere else—marsupials, which raise their young in pouches, and monotremes, which lay eggs. Remarkably, these creatures have evolved to fill niches similar to those of their counterparts elsewhere.

The small tasmanian devil is now almost the only marsupial hunter, although there was once a marsupial lion.

Bandicoots and **numbats** (banded anteaters) are insect eaters, with long snouts and strong digging claws.

The marsupial mole is a blind burrowing animal with strong front paws for tunneling through the ground.

Marsupial niches

Marsupials first evolved 100 million years ago and once lived all over the world. Placental mammals, whose young are born more fully developed, were thought to have evolved later, and to have driven marsupials into extinction almost everywhere but Australia, where they survived in isolation. Recent finds of 115-million-year-old placental mammal fossils in Australia, and analysis of DNA from both kinds of mammal, suggest that they may have lived alongside each other for millions of years. Whatever the truth, it is clear that the Australian marsupials have evolved to fill roles in the habitat similar to those occupied by their counterparts elsewhere. This is known as convergent evolution.

Carnivores

Leopard
Big cats and wild dogs are the large predators of the placental world. They now have no marsupial counterparts.

Insectivores

Giant pangolin
Placental anteaters like giant pangolins and anteaters also have long snouts and strong digging claws.

Burrowers

Giant golden mole
Placental moles are remarkably similar to their marsupial counterparts.

Grassland adaptations: Big feet for hopping

Placental grazing animals run on four thin legs to escape predators, whereas many marsupials hop on strong hind legs and feet (and tails). The hind legs of a red kangaroo are roughly 10 times the size of its front legs. When moving slowly, kangaroos use all four legs, but when they need to move fast, they rise up on their hind legs and hop. It takes a lot of energy to start hopping, but very little energy is needed to hop faster. In contrast, four-legged mammals need more and more energy as they run faster.

The inner toes of the kangaroo family have grown especially large and strong.

Besides marsupials, many rodents hop, including the northern hopping mouse and the U.S.'s kangaroo rat. They also have long inner toes.

Rock wallaby

Northern hopping mouse

Wombats fill a similar niche to marmots and badgers but grow larger because there is no competition. Oddly, there are no large marsupial foragers.

Koalas, possums, and cuscuses are tree-dwelling marsupials that feed on vegetation.

The red kangaroo is a big grazing animal like antelope, deer, and buffalo, but is strikingly different. It has few predators to avoid and relies on hopping on its two big feet, rather than running, to escape.

Herbivores

Elephant
Elsewhere in the world, there are not only small foragers like badgers, but also giants like elephants.

Tree-dwellers

Vervet monkey
Squirrels, marmosets, and monkeys, such as the vervet, are the placental equivalent of marsupial tree-dwellers.

Grazers

African buffalo
In the rest of the world, big grazers like the buffalo have developed long legs and hooves—and safety in numbers—to escape from predators.

Mallee fowl

The mallee fowl is a large ground bird that builds a compost heap to keep its eggs warm. In fall, the male digs a hole (pictured) and fills it with vegetation. When it rains in spring, the vegetation rots and heats up. The female then lays her egg, which is kept warm by heat from the compost. The male keeps testing the temperature, and adds sand to save heat if it is too cold, or opens up the mound to let out heat if it is too hot. This way the mound stays at exactly 91°F (33°C), which is why the mallee is known as "the thermometer bird."

21

Wildlife at risk!

Bridled nail-tailed wallaby
The bridled nail-tailed wallaby gets its name from the little nail of bone on the end of its tail. Once common, it was hunted as a pest and for its fur so vigorously that by 1960 it was believed to be extinct. A few were rediscovered in 1973 in Queensland, but it is still very rare.

Numbat
Unlike other marsupials, numbats, or banded anteaters, are active during the day. These small creatures consume up to 20,000 termites a day. Many have been killed by foxes introduced from Europe and now survive only in the Wandoo bushland of southwest Australia.

The cassowary
The cassowary is a large flightless bird of Australia's rain forests. It plays a crucial role in distributing the seeds of 150 species of forest plants, but loss of its habitats and road accidents have severely reduced its numbers.

Tropical rain forests

Where there is enough rain in the tropics, forests grow—and the combination of year-round warmth and moisture makes tropical rain forests the lushest, greenest, densest, and most richly varied natural habitats on Earth.

•

Tropical rain forests cover barely six percent of the world's land surface. Yet they contain 50 percent of its plant and animal species. Some scientists think it may be as much as 90 percent. Indeed, more species of amphibian, bird, insect, mammal, and reptile live here than in all the other habitats put together. One study found more species of ant living on a single rain forest stump than in all of the British Isles.

•

Yet rain forests are incredibly fragile environments—partly because the plants and animals depend on each other to an exceptional degree. Here, almost all trees rely on animals to disperse their seeds; elsewhere, dispersal by the wind is the most common method. As more and more rain forest is affected by human activity, the very existence of thousands of animal species is endangered.

Where are tropical rain forests?

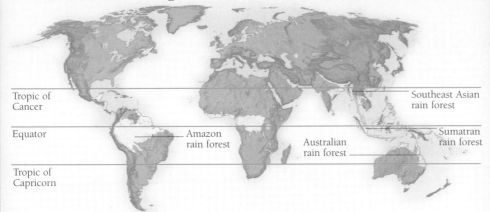

Tropic of Cancer

Southeast Asian rain forest

Equator — Amazon rain forest

Australian rain forest

Sumatran rain forest

Tropic of Capricorn

Comparing tropical rain forests

| Brazil nut, sacupaia trees | Myrtle, laurel bushes | Lianas, vines | Bromeliads, orchids | Mahogany, iroko trees | Cacao | Raffia, sisal | Fungi |

South America
The Amazon rain forest has a rich variety of trees both large (e.g. rubber, Brazil nut, silk-cotton, sacupaia, and sucupir), and small (myrtle, laurel, bignonia). They are all covered with lianas and epiphytes (plants that grow on other plants), such as orchids and bromeliads.

Epiphytes | Tea trees | Strangler figs | Durian, mango

Africa
African rain forests are less varied than those of the Amazon. The trees are large hardwoods, such as mahogany, iroko, and sapele, and smaller trees such as cacao. Beneath them grow fibrous plants including raffia, sisal, and numerous fungi.

Australasia and Asia
Southeast Asian rain forests are dominated by huge dipterocarps (tea trees) along with teak and ironwood, under which grow a wealth of small trees, including fruits, such as durian, lychees, mangoes, and mulberries. Trees are covered with mosses, epiphytes, and climbers, such as strangler figs. Exotic flowers, such as rafflesia and titan arum, grow on the ground.

Tropical rain forest environments

Rain forests are typically hot and steamy. Temperatures rarely rise above 93°F (34°C) nor fall below 68°F (20°C). There is no dry season and rain falls most afternoons. The rainfall totals over 4 in (100 mm) of rain each month.

Sun and rain
Rainfall month by month and average daily temperature is shown for the Uaupés River, in the Amazon. The hottest month is often little more than 3–9°F (2–5°C) warmer than the coldest month.

Treetop pools
The dense canopy of leaves catches much of the rain. At least half the water reaching the ground is later given off by the leaves in transpiration. The trees are so damp that special "air plants" live on them. Some frogs even live in pools that collect on these air plants.

Thunderclouds
Most rain in the rain forest comes in thundershowers, which occur at least 200 days a year. Tropical warmth and humidity combine to build up huge thunderclouds each morning, which release their rain in the afternoon.

Australasian and Asian rain forests

Unlike the immense Amazon rain forest, the tropical rain forests of southern Asia, Indonesia, and Australia occupy quite small areas; and many of the larger animals, such as elephants, rhinos, and tigers, are under threat from human activity. Nevertheless, these forests remain home to an incredibly rich diversity of wildlife, including some of the world's most colorful birds and butterflies.

Wallace's Line
West of a line called "Wallace's Line," in S. E. Asia, there are deer, monkeys, pigs, cats, elephants, and rhinos. To the east, in New Guinea and Australia, are marsupials like possums, cuscuses, tree-kangaroos, and bandicoots.

Ganges forest
is much depleted but is still home to tigers, rhinos, elephants, and gaurs.

Malaysia
is home to 193 species of mammal, including elephants, tigers, rhinos, clouded leopards, and sun bears.

Borneo
has a rich rain forest fauna, including 380 bird species, such as white-rumped shamas, and 13 primate species, such as orangutans and macaques.

Birds
In Asia, the forest canopy is full of colorful hornbills, lorikeets, sunbirds, leafbirds, and fairy bluebirds, along with wood swallows and tree swifts. On the ground run peafowl, bleeding heart doves, ground doves, pheasant, pittas, crowned pigeons, and flowerpeckers.

King of Saxony's bird of paradise
This is one of 43 kinds of dazzling birds of paradise that live in the forest canopy mostly in New Guinea and Australia, along with many other colorful birds, such as king parrots, fruit doves, and cuckoo-shrikes. The male has two long feathers growing from his head. During courtship, he holds them high and bounces up and down. As a female nears, he sweeps them before her.

Pileated gibbon
Gibbons are the smallest of the apes, but they can move through the trees with astonishing speed and agility. They have very long arms, which they use to swing over 10 ft (3 m) in a single movement. There are six species of gibbon, the largest of which is the siamang of Malaysia and Sumatra, famous for its loud whooping cry.

Primates
There are no primates in Australia, but many in southeast Asia. Best known are apes, such as gibbons and orangutans. There are also monkeys, such as rhesus macaques, 18 species of langur, and the big-nosed proboscis monkey.

Flying fox
This is actually a bat, called the greater fruit bat. It has the largest wings of any bat, spanning 6 ft (1.8 m). Unlike some bats, fruit bats have large eyes and see well in black and white, but they find the fruit they eat mainly by smell. By day, they roost in trees, taking flight only at dusk.

Insects
Besides countless tiny insects, such as termites, there are many huge ones, including giant stick insects, walking leaves, giant atlas beetles, beautiful luna moths, and birdwing butterflies.

Birdwing butterfly
The Queen Alexandra's birdwing of southeast Papua New Guinea is the world's biggest butterfly, over 12 in (30.5 cm) across.

Flying creatures
As well as numerous kinds of bat, the forests of Australasia have a unique range of gliding animals, such as flying squirrels, snakes and frogs, and geckos. The most skillful are the gliding lemurs or colugos which can glide huge distances.

Reptiles and amphibians

Australasian rain forests are home to many snakes, such as venomous spitting cobras and taipans, and constrictors like the green and reticulated pythons. There are also hundreds of species of lizard, including many agamids and monitors, such as Salvador's.

Anoa (dwarf buffalo)

Anoas are small buffaloes, standing barely 40 in (1 m) at the shoulder. They have almost no hair and enjoy bathing and wallowing in mud. They were once common on the Indonesian island of Sulawesi, but they are hunted for their horns, hide, and meat. As farms have spread, the survivors have retreated into inaccessible, swampy forest.

Browsers and foragers

The biggest browsers and foragers are Asian elephants, but they are now very rare in the wild. So, too, are the various species of rhino found on different Indonesian islands, such as the Javan and Sumatran. Most common are wild hogs, piglike babirusas, and tapirs.

Grazing mammals

There are many small deer, including the tiny mouse deer (chevrotain), musk deer, tufted deer, Indian muntjac, sambar deer, and barking deer. The larger grazers are buffaloes and oxen, such as anoa and banteng. Tree kangaroos are found in Australian forests.

Komodo dragon

The Komodo dragon lives on the island of Komodo and nearby islands in Indonesia. It is the largest living lizard, growing up to 10 ft (3 m) long, and is strong enough to overpower and eat deer, wild boar, and water buffalo. Despite its bulk, it can run surprisingly fast to catch its prey, and can swim and even climb trees. It spends the night in a small hole it has dug.

Malayan tapir

Malayan tapirs have a short, flexible nose that they use to help them feed on water plants. They usually live near water and swim well.

New Guinea
Among over 80 species of native mammals here, 44 are found nowhere else, including dusky pademelons and bats, such as the mastiff.

Queensland forests
Here live many marsupials, including tree kangaroos and possums, and birds, such as cassowaries.

Small mammals

Among the many small mammals that live in the Australasian rain forests are marsupials, such as echidnas, bandicoots, and cuscuses. There are also numerous rodents, brush-tailed porcupines, tree shrews, and bulbuls.

Tree shrew

Tree shrews are small creatures that live in the southeast Asian rain forests. They scamper up and down trees like squirrels, but spend much of their time on the ground, feeding on ants, spiders, and seeds. Some scientists classify them as primates, others as insectivores (like shrews).

Predatory mammals

There are still tigers and leopards in the forests of southern Asia, Sumatra, and Java, but they are rare. The clouded leopard is also rare, with only about 10,000 left. Small civets, such as the masked palm civet, are still quite common.

Clouded leopard

The clouded leopard is one of the most agile of all cat climbers. It can hang from branches with just its back feet, and run up and down trees like a squirrel. It often hunts by pouncing from trees and can kill prey, such as birds, pigs, and small deer, with a single bite from its very long canine teeth. It cannot roar, but it is one of the few big cats that can actually purr.

Jungle survival

Tropical rain forests contain an incredible range of animals. In an area of just 39 sq miles (100 sq km), there may be more than 400 different bird species, 150 kinds of reptile and amphibian, 125 types of mammal, and tens of thousands of different insects. With this range of wildlife, there is a remarkable degree of interdependence. Rain forests are among the most stable and ancient of environments, and, over millions of years, a complex web of food relationships has developed between different animals. and also between plants and animals.

Flies and beetles

Sheath-tailed bat

Masked palm civet

Water monitor lizard

Ants

Moon rat

Asian rain forest food chains

At the top of the food chains are the large predators. Big cats, such as leopards, and wild dogs like the dhole stalk the jungle floor. In the lower branches, there are smaller cats like the masked palm civet and clouded leopard, and snakes, such as the green python. In the canopy, there are snakes like the flying snake, and predatory birds, such as the bat hawk, crested serpent eagle, and the variable goshawk. Below each of these top predators is a food chain of species feeding upon species.

Forest floor animals
Dholes hunt in packs to bring down animals as big as banteng and water buffalo as well as small deer like mouse deer. Small predators, such as the moon rat and water monitor lizard, feed mainly on insects, such as ants and termites, that crawl on the forest floor.

Banteng

Dhole | Tree shrew | Mouse deer

Rain forest adaptation: Flying and gliding

In the rain forests of southeast Asia, a number of canopy animals have developed the ability to take to the air, both to move in the canopy and to escape predators. They are not true fliers, but have grown winglike extensions to help them glide from tree to tree, or to the ground. They include the Rhacophorus flying frogs, which can glide 165 ft (50 m), the flying squirrels, such as Thomas's and the black flying squirrel, and the Ptychozoon flying geckos.

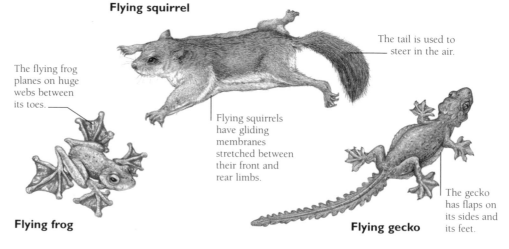

Flying squirrel

The tail is used to steer in the air.

The flying frog planes on huge webs between its toes.

Flying squirrels have gliding membranes stretched between their front and rear limbs.

Flying frog

The gecko has flaps on its sides and its feet.

Flying gecko

Bat hawk　　Bar-winged flycatcher　　Crested serpent eagle

Green tree
python

Shrews, snakes, and cats
Green tree pythons loop themselves silently around tree branches to wait for prey, such as tree shrews, mouse deer, and civets, which they suffocate in their coils. The shrews feed on insects and fruit. The masked palm civet hunts at night for rodents and lizards.

Bats and flycatchers
Bats like the sheath-tailed bat, and birds like the bar-winged flycatcher catch flies in midair high above the forest floor in the canopy. Bats hunt by night and birds mostly by day. Both are preyed on by bat hawks.

Birds of prey
High up in the treetops, birds of prey hunt. Bat hawks swoop on birds, such as flycatchers, swallows, and swiftlets. They also prey on bats, gliding at dusk, snapping them up as they emerge from their bat caves. Crested serpent eagles feed on reptiles, such as tree snakes. They usually watch their prey from branches in the canopy, then dive through the branches to strike.

Sumatran tiger
Sumatran tigers are the smallest of all tigers, with a very dark coat and striped forelegs. They eat mostly sambar and other deer and wild pigs, but will occasionally kill a rhino calf. Like all tigers, they rely on ambushing their prey, so they prefer to live in the densest parts of the forest, where they can find cover. There are now only about 400 of them left in the wild in five national parks on Sumatra. There are just over 200 in zoos around the world.

Wildlife at risk!

Orangutan
Orangutans are the largest of the tree-dwelling apes, with arms over 6½ ft (2 m) long. They once lived all over south China and southeast Asia. But their forest habitats have been so reduced that there are now just 12,000 individuals on Borneo and 7,000 on Sumatra.

Javan rhinoceros
The one-horned Javan rhinoceros is the rarest of all the five species of rhino. Less than 60 individuals survive altogether in just two locations—in Indonesia and in Vietnam. The very similar Sumatran rhinoceros is only slightly more numerous.

Gurney's pitta
Gurney's pitta is a small ground bird that lives in the forests of Thailand and Burma. The almost total destruction of its lowland forest habitat means there are fewer than 25 pairs remaining, and it is now the subject of a major conservation drive.

27

Sumatran rain forest

Long, narrow, and mountainous, Sumatra
is Indonesia's largest island, stretching
almost 1,250 miles (2,000 km) through
the Indian Ocean. Although much of its
lush lowland forest has been cleared, the highlands are
still blanketed with some of the world's most spectacular
rain forests. Here, in the steamy tropical air and
monsoon rain grows an astonishing profusion of plants.
Giant tea trees festooned with creepers tower above the
canopy, along with durian, sandalwood, teak, ironwood,
and many other trees. Around their trunks grow some
40,000 species of flowers, including rafflesia, the
world's biggest flower—almost 3 ft (1 m) across
and with a strong, pervasive smell like rotting meat.

Dusk in the Sumatran rain forest

High up in the dense canopy of trees in Sumatra's rain forest, branches are dappled with light from the setting sun, while far below, the forest floor is already shrouded in gloom. Water from the afternoon rain spills from pitcher plants and drips from dark green leaves. This is the time when the forest begins to buzz with activity as animals that feed at dusk and at night, such as fruit bats, emerge.

•

In among the branches, scores of rainbow lorikeets, rufous fantails, hornbills, flycatchers, and other colorful birds are still flying to and fro searching for fruit and insects. A flying squirrel glides effortlessly through the moist air. A mother orangutan sits on a lower branch clutching her baby while her partner swings off to search for food. Nearby a trio of large-nosed proboscis monkeys chatter noisily.

•

A reticulated python slithers along a bough, looking for prey, while a clouded leopard watches silently for unwary mouse deer (chevrotain). In the undergrowth, piglike babirusa are foraging, while in the distance, a pair of elephants stand quietly browsing.

KEY

1 Reticulated python	**13** Mouse deer
2 Orangutan	**14** Atlas moth
3 Male orangutan	**15** Cassowary
4 Clouded leopard, slow loris	**16** Monitor lizard
5 Babirusa	**17** Tiger, tapir
6 King cobra	**18** Asian elephant
7 Birdwing butterfly	**19** Proboscis monkey
8 Orb spider	**20** Rainbow lorikeet
9 Stag beetle	**21** Flying squirrel
10 Rafflesia	**22** Rhinoceros hornbill
11 Rufous fantail	**23** Brahminy kite
12 Jungle fowl	**24** Tarsier

South American rain forests

Choco-Darien
Separated by the Andes from the Amazon, this wet region has its own rich array of creatures, including Baird's tapir, Geoffrey's tamarin, and the toucan barbet.

The Amazon rain forest is by far the largest continuous area of rain forest in the world—and home to a wider variety of different creatures than almost all the rest of the world put together. There are tens of thousands of known species here—from soldier ants and tiny hummingbirds to giant beetles and the biggest snakes in the world—and there are many more that have yet to be identified.

ANDES MOUNTAINS

PACIFIC OCEAN

River Amazon

Southwest Amazon
The forest has an extraordinary number of birds and mammals, including red uakari monkeys, ocelots, capybaras, and giant otters.

River mammals

The Amazon river has its own unique range of mammals, including dolphins and sea cows (manatees), which look like seals but are unrelated. There are also rodents, such as the coypu and capybara—the world's largest rodent, which weighs up to 176 lb (80 kg).

Anaconda

The anaconda is one of the world's biggest snakes, sometimes growing up to 30 ft (9 m) long. Despite their size, anacondas feed mainly on small birds and animals. They catch their prey by lurking in murky waters, waiting. They are not poisonous, but kill by constriction—wrapping their coils around the victim and squeezing until it suffocates.

Amazon dolphin (bouto)

The Amazon river dolphin or bouto is the largest freshwater dolphin, reaching 8½ ft (2.6 m) in length. As it matures, it often turns vivid pink in color, but it is usually blue-gray like other dolphins. Unusually, for a dolphin, it can bend its neck to turn its head in any direction. It often swims upside down to see the riverbed.

Reptiles

The Amazon is one of the richest of all habitats for reptiles. Not only are there crocodile-like caimans and various turtles, such as the Arrau river turtle and the matamata, but also many snakes, such as the emerald tree boa, the vine snake, and the anaconda.

Woolly spider monkey

The woolly spider monkey is the largest monkey in the Amazon, and lives in the tops of the highest trees. It can hang by its tail, and resembles a spider as it hangs upside down with all four limbs and tail grasping a branch. Unlike nearly all other monkeys, it has no thumb.

Amphibians

There is little standing water in the rain forest, yet many amphibians live here. Rain frogs live by small puddles, and many tree frogs live by pools in treetop plants. Toads, such as leaf and marine toads, live in damp leaf litter, as do salamanders and legless caecilians.

Poison arrow frog

In the rain forests of South and Central America live a number of different poison arrow frogs. These brightly colored tree frogs get their name from the deadly "batrachotoxin" poison secreted by their skin, which native hunters put on their arrow tips. The poison from the skin of one frog is enough to kill 100 people.

Primates

The Amazon's monkeys include spider monkeys, howlers, titis, capuchins, sakis, and uakaris, and over 30 kinds of small marmoset and tamarin. Unlike monkeys elsewhere, Amazon monkeys have flat, wide noses.

Insects

More than one million insect species are thought to live in the Amazon, including ants, fireflies, bees, cicadas, centipedes, and many kinds of vividly colored butterflies.

Acteon beetle

Of all the South American rain forest's many beetle species, none is more spectacular than the acteon beetle (*Megasoma acteon*). This is the world's biggest beetle, growing up to 3½ in (9 cm) long and 2 in (5 cm) wide—bigger even than Africa's giant goliath beetle.

Birds of the air

The Amazon air is constantly filled with the sound of myriad birds—colorful parrots, macaws, and parakeets, noisy caciques, elegant hoatzins, quetzals, jewel-like hummingbirds, giant-billed toucans, and numerous small birds, such as antbirds and woodpeckers.

Negro-Branco forests
Here in the remote heart of the Amazon, saki monkeys and jaguars and many other rare animals survive—and even the giant ground sloth may not be a myth.

Ground birds

The dense vegetation on the Amazon forest floor provides good cover for a range of ground birds, including elegant sunbitterns, quail doves, quails, nightjars, and 47 kinds of henlike tinamous. Waterbirds include cormorants, spoonbills, and ibises.

Great curassow

Curassows are a family of 50 American rain forest species that includes chacalacas and guans. Great curassows are about 40 in (1 m) long. They roost and nest in trees, but spend a great deal of time on the ground searching for fruit, leaves, and berries. The males have a loud, booming call that they use to attract females and threaten other males.

Predatory mammals

The largest predators are the big cats—jaguars, ocelots, and pumas. Jaguars and ocelots are now rare, though pumas are more common toward the Andes mountains. Smaller predators include raccoonlike coatis, ferretlike grisons, and weasels.

Three-toed sloth

Sloths are leaf-eating creatures that hang upside down in trees from their hooklike claws. They hang so securely they can sleep like this—and may even remain hanging like this after they die. They move so little that green algae grows on their fur, giving them a greenish tinge.

Herbivores; small mammals

Besides tiny deer and piglike peccaries and tapirs, there is an abundance of small mammals, including many rodents, such as agoutis, capybaras, pacas, and porcupines, a range of anteaters and sloths, the kinkajou and many bats, including the blood-drinking vampire.

Ocelot

The ocelot sleeps by day in a tree or in dense vegetation, and emerges at night to hunt on the ground for small mammals, such as deer and peccaries. Its favorite food is agouti. Ocelots are among the most beautiful of cats, and they have been hunted intensively for their pelts. Hunting is now banned, but there are very few ocelots left.

Toco Toucan

The toco toucan is the largest of the 41 species of toucans. The toco's bill can grow up to 8 in (20 cm) long—almost as long as its body. No one knows quite why it has such a large, colorful bill. It may be to attract a mate, or to gather hard-to-reach fruit. The toucan seizes fruit with the tip of its bill, then throws back its head to toss the fruit into its mouth.

Fish

There are over 1,500 known species of fish in the Amazon—and many more as yet unidentified. They include piranhas, hatchet fish, knife fish, arapaimas, and the pirarucu (the world's largest freshwater fish).

Electric eel

Electric eels are long fish that live in muddy rivers in the Amazon basin. With special muscle cells, they can generate a 650-volt electric shock—enough to stun a human. The electricity is used to detect underwater objects, signal to other eels, and stun or kill the fish they prey on.

Living on trees

It is a long way down from the tops of the trees in the Amazon rain forest—often 165 ft (50 m) or more—and the leaves and branches grow so densely that little sunlight ever penetrates to the ground. High in the treetop canopy, there is sun and rain and breezy air. Far below on the forest floor, it is still, humid, and perpetually gloomy. So striking is the difference in conditions that there are often distinct layers down through the trees. Each layer forms a different habitat, with its own range of plants and animals, each adapted to its own particular world.

Rain forest adaptations: Colorful plumage

Many of the world's most beautifully colored birds live in rain forests. In the Amazon, there are exotic cotingas and macaws, jewel-like hummingbirds and many others. Colored plumage may help birds find each other in dense jungle foliage. Male birds are especially vivid to attract females, which are often drab in comparison.

The iridescently hued hummingbird is one of 319 species of hummingbird. So gemlike are these tiny birds that in the 1800s they were actually made into jewelry.

Macaws like the scarlet macaw are the biggest and most brightly colored of all parrots.

The Andean cock-of-the-rock is the best known of over 90 kinds of cotinga. The male is bright red, but the female is brown. Though cotinga is Indian for "whitewashed" from the white bellbird cotinga, many cotingas have bright plumage.

65–165 ft (20–50 m): Canopy layer

The canopy is the lush green layer of tree crowns, bathed with sun and rain and teeming with life, nourished by the abundance of fruit and nuts that grow here. Most animals in the canopy spend all their lives up there, and are well adapted to treetop life. There are fliers, such as birds, bats, and butterflies; gliders like some squirrels; and climbers, such as monkeys, sloths, beetles, ants, and spiders.

Forest floor

Large mammals, such as peccaries, and deer and birds, such as curassows, feed on the vegetation on the forest floor, foraging over a wide area rather than climbing or flying. Smaller mammals feed on insects and plant matter. Worms, centipedes, ants, termites, cockroaches, and a host of other tiny creatures live in the dank layer of rotting vegetation on the forest floor.

Layers of the rain forest

There are typically four layers in the rain forest—the forest floor; the "understory" of small trees, tree trunks, and shrubs; the "canopy" of tree crowns; and the "emergent" layer of tall trees rising above the canopy. Sometimes, the pattern of layers is disturbed by natural events. As a tree grows old and falls, for instance, it may pull with it many others tied to it by vines, creating a clearing; new trees will grow in the clearing, and the layers are eventually reestablished.

Female blue morpho butterfly

Vulturine parrot

Great jacamar

Vampire bat

Hoatzin

Tarantula

Leafcutter ants

Ruddy quail dove

Pudu

White-lipped peccary

Sunbittern

Termites, cockroaches, beetles, centipedes, millipedes, earthworms

Harpy eagle

Spider monkey

Blue morpho butterfly

Two-lined bat

Howler monkey

Three-toed sloth

Toucan

Prehensile-tailed porcupine

Emerald tree boa

Olingo

Hummingbird

White fronted nun bird

St Vincent Amazon parrot

Golden toad

Great curassow

Kinkajou

Poison arrow frog

Ocelot

Upper Amazon porcupine

115–230 ft (35–70 m): Emergent layer

The tallest trees may tower 230 ft (70 m) into the sunlight. Here agile flying creatures—mainly insect-eating birds and bats—swoop on their prey in midair. The birds and bats, in turn, are hunted by big birds of prey, such as the harpy eagle. Spider monkeys may climb up for fruit.

15–65 ft (4.5–20 m): Understory layer

This is the lower layer of small trees and shrubs, and tangled vines used by climbing creatures. Little sunlight gets down here and many leaves are colored dark green or red, to make the best use of the available light. Birds, bats, monkeys, squirrels, and many kinds of snake live here. There are frogs, too, finding the water to lay their eggs in pools caught by plants high up in the trees.

Blue morpho

The blue morphos that live in the forest canopy are large butterflies, up to 6½ in (16.5 cm) across. The tops of their wings flash iridescent blue in the sunlight as they fly, but the undersides of the wings are brown, which keeps them hidden when they rest with their wings folded up.

Wildlife at risk!

Resplendent quetzal
The 2 ft- (60 cm-) long tail feathers of the quetzal were worn by Aztec kings. Quetzals were once common, but the expansion of farming has made the wild avocados on which they feed scarce. The birds now live only in remote areas of Central American cloud forest.

Cottontop tamarin
Tamarins are small monkeys that feed on fruit, insects, and frogs. Their forest habitat has been reduced, and tens of thousands of tamarins were taken to the U.S. for medical research. The cottontop tamarin is now one of the world's most endangered primates.

Forest clearance
Rain forest is being destroyed at an alarming rate and, with it, the habitat of countless creatures. An area of Amazon forest as big as Scotland is lost each year, as trees are cut down for timber or simply burned to clear the land. Once rain forest is cleared, it is unlikely to recover. The forest's nutrients are locked into the trees, not the soil, and once the trees go, so do the nutrients.

African rain forests

Although the African rain forests have fewer species than those of South America and Asia, they are still an astonishingly rich habitat.

Among the giant hardwood trees of the Congo rain forest lives a huge variety of creatures, including monkeys, apes, and smaller primates that use their gripping hands and feet to move through the trees with amazing agility.

Eastern Guinea
Much reduced in size, this forest is still home to many monkeys, such as sooty mangabeys and dianas, and also rare pygmy hippos.

Okapi

With their striped legs, okapis were thought to be related to zebras when they were first discovered by European explorers in the Congo in 1901. In fact, they are related to giraffes. Like giraffes, okapis have long tongues which they can use to twist and pull leaves from trees—and also to lick clean their own eyes.

Dzanga Sangha, central Africa
One of the last areas of untouched rain forest, this is the home of rare forest elephants, bonobos, and lowland gorillas.

Madagascar
Cut off from mainland Africa 150 million years ago, this island has unique fauna, including lemurs and ayes-ayes.

Foraging mammals
The largest animals in the African rain forest are okapis and elephants, both of which can browse on leaves some way above the ground. Small foragers include the pygmy hippo and hogs, such as the red river hog and the giant forest hog, the world's biggest pig.

Colobus monkey

Agile colobus monkeys are known as "leaf-monkeys" because they eat mainly leaves. The Angolan black and white is one of nine species. In the past it was killed for its long, silky hair and it is now quite rare.

Oleander hawk (sphinx) moth

This is the most spectacular hawk moth. Big and a strong flier, it hovers in front of flowers like a hummingbird, to suck the nectar with its long proboscis.

Small mammals
Among the many small mammals living in the rain forest are tree hyraxes, the African brush-tailed porcupine, and tree pangolins. Tree pangolins are similar to anteaters, but are covered with an armor of scales. They spend most of their lives in trees.

Armored shrew

The armored shrew has an incredibly strong spine reinforced by bony flanges and rods. Mangbetu natives in the Congo call it the "hero shrew" because they can stand on its back without breaking it! In other respects it is much like other shrews, except that it moves slowly.

Insects
Like all rain forests, Africa's teem with insects, including many species of beetle (such as the giant goliath beetle), ant, termite, fly, and cockroach, including the huge Madagascar hissing cockroach that forces air out of its body noisily in order to alarm predators.

Monkeys and apes
Monkeys and apes are kings of Africa's forests, moving freely through the trees in search of fruit, leaves, and insects. Here live three of the four great apes: chimpanzee, bonobo, and gorilla. (The fourth is the orangutan.) Monkeys include monas, mangabeys, and colobus.

Birds of the air

African rain forests are home to dozens of species of hornbills (Africa's equivalent of Amazonian toucans), scores of colorful parrots and lovebirds, plus barbets, turacos, bulbuls, orioles, and blue rollers.

Red-crested turaco

Turacos spend much of their lives high up in the trees, but they are quite poor fliers. Instead, they climb and run along branches with the nimbleness of a squirrel. The beautiful plumage of the red-crested turaco is still highly prized by African tribal chiefs.

Ground birds

The largest birds in the African rain forest are those that forage on the ground for seeds, shoots, tubers, and berries. The biggest is the spectacular Congo peafowl, but the vulturine guinea fowl and the red-necked francolin are also very large birds. Less conspicuous are ground-nesters, such as the standard-winged nightjar.

Congo peafowl

The Congo peafowl is the only pheasant found in Africa and its discovery in 1936 caused a sensation, for pheasants were thought to be exclusively Eurasian. They are rare, shy birds that roam the forest floor in pairs or family groups. It is silent during the day, but when it roosts in trees at night, it screeches loudly.

Aye-aye

The Madagascan aye-aye is a nocturnal creature with long, slender fingers. It uses its long third finger to tap on tree trunks to find insects, listening for movement with its super-sensitive ears. It then probes with the same finger to draw out the insect. During the day, aye-ayes hide in treetop nests of twigs.

Grazing mammals

Africa's grassland grazers rely on speed and stamina to escape from predators. Rain forest grazers escape by being elusive. Antelopes are either small enough to dart into hiding, like royals and duikers, or are camouflaged like the bongos.

Reptiles and amphibians

Africa's rain forest is home to *Rana Goliath*, the world's biggest frog—at 12 in (30.5 cm) tall it is almost as big as the royal antelope. There are also colorful sedge frogs, chameleons, and lizards, such as Nile monitors. Snakes include pythons and tree cobras.

Small primates: prosimians

Relatives of monkeys and apes, prosimians are small primates with big eyes and long tails. Like all primates, they use their hands and feet to climb. Pottos and bush babies live in all African rain forests, but lemurs, aye-ayes, and indris live only on Madagascar.

Royal antelope

The royal antelope of the west African rain forest is the world's smallest hoofed animal—less than 12 in (30.5 cm) high and with pencil-thin legs. It is a shy creature, able to vanish quickly when spotted—and can bound nearly 10 ft (3 m). It is famed in local folklore for its speed and its wisdom.

Eastern green mamba

The eastern green mamba is a long, slender snake that slithers along branches hunting for lizards and small birds. It is not quite as deadly as its savanna relative, the black mamba, but its poison is still lethal to humans. In the breeding season, males engage in ritual fights for females, twisting their bodies around each other.

African palm civet

Civets look a little like cats, but have more pointed snouts, bushier tails, and shorter legs. They mark out their territory and attract a mate using scent from glands near the base of the tail. The base of this scent is musk, which is used to make perfumes. The African palm civet is nocturnal and hunts in the forest canopy for insects, lizards, and small mammals.

Predatory mammals

In treetops, crowned eagles are major predators; in branches, pythons are. Only near ground are mammals the main hunters. Here the leopard is the top predator, hunting young antelopes, monkeys, and apes.

Moving through trees

Moving through branches high above the ground is very different from moving along the ground. So many rain forest animals have developed special skills for what zoologists call "arboreal locomotion," including leaping, climbing, swinging, and gliding. Tree frogs have special pads on their toes that help them as they climb. Woodpeckers, treecreepers, and other birds have clawed feet for clinging. Squirrels and other small mammals climb with the help of claws, too. But the best climbers are monkeys, apes, and smaller primates who climb, leap, and swing with astonishing agility.

Gorilla

The gorilla is the biggest of all the apes, standing 6½ ft (2 m) tall and weighing up to 500 lb (230 kg). Despite its fierce appearance, it is a shy, gentle creature that eats only leaves and shoots. Males thump their chests to warn off intruders. Gorillas have long arms suitable for swinging, but they never do so, spending much of their time on the ground, walking on all fours on their knuckles. They climb trees at night to find a place safe from leopards, their only enemy apart from humans.

Rain forest adaptation: Hands for gripping

All primates are well adapted to living in trees and nearly all have hands with fingers and feet with toes for gripping branches—except for humans (whose feet cannot grip) and tree shrews (that cannot grip with their hands). American monkeys have a short thumb like every other finger. But African and Asian monkeys and apes have an opposable thumb— that is, a thumb that can bend the opposite way to the fingers to provide a very precise grip. With this precision grip, some apes can use tools, such as sticks and stones, very effectively to get food. In human hands, the opposable thumb is highly developed.

Short opposable thumb for branch swinging.

New World monkey with short thumb.

Spider monkey

Large opposable thumb for very precise grip.

Ape: gibbon

Ape: gorilla

Short opposable thumb for walking on palms.

Monkey: macaque

Capuchin: climbing and leaping

Black spider monkey: leaping and New World brachiation (with prehensile tail)

South America

All monkeys climb using their four long limbs. This way of moving is called quadrapedalism. Capuchins and many other American monkeys, such as sakis, titis, and marmosets, move like this—climbing, springing, and running along branches with amazing agility. Some American (New World) monkeys, like spiders and howlers, also have extra help to mobility possessed by no Asian and African (Old World) monkey—a prehensile or gripping tail. This tail is like an extra limb, giving enough support for monkeys to swing from branch to branch on their arms, a technique called "New World semi-brachiation."

Galago: leaping

Mangabey: climbing and leaping

Colobus: leaping and Old World semi-brachiation

Chimpanzee: Old World brachiation and running

Mandrill: quadrapedal on the ground

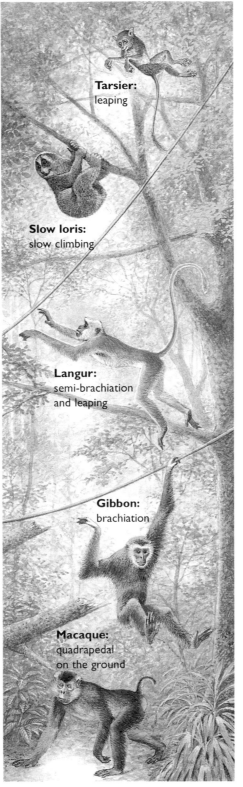

Tarsier: leaping

Slow loris: slow climbing

Langur: semi-brachiation and leaping

Gibbon: brachiation

Macaque: quadrapedal on the ground

Africa

Like American monkeys, African monkeys move on all four limbs—some climbing and others, like mandrills, running on the ground. A few, like mangabeys, are slow climbers, but most African monkeys are more agile than American monkeys. The colobus is a great leaper. The colobus and a few others may also swing from their arms ("Old World semibrachiation"). Prosimians (small primates like bush babies) cling vertically to tree trunks and may leap. Apes, such as chimpanzees, have long arms and swing properly (brachiation), though they are too big to climb high. Gorillas rarely climb at all and walk on their knuckles.

Asia

Asian monkeys move on all fours like American and African monkeys. Some, like macaques, run on the ground, only rarely climbing trees. Others, like langurs, move easily through the trees using their tail as a balance, making leaps of 33 ft (10 m). Asia's two apes—the gibbon and orangutan—both brachiate (swing from their arms). While orangutans swing only when young and climb slowly when older, gibbons are the greatest of all swingers, moving from branch to branch on their long arms with amazing agility. Prosimians are clingers and leapers, but while lorises climb slowly, tarsiers leap energetically.

Wildlife at risk!

Pygmy hippopotamus
Pygmy hippos are only about the size of a large pig. They live in forests in west Africa and spend less of their time in the water than their large relatives. Although hunting is banned, many local people still poach them for food and there are now only a few thousand left.

Endangered chimps
Lively and intelligent, chimpanzees are our closest relatives in the animal world. Over 100,000 survive in the wild in west and central Africa, but numbers are dwindling as they are hunted for food, captured for medical research, and their habitat is slowly eroded.

Big game hunters
In the past, big game hunters came to Africa to hunt large mammals like lions and rhinos for sport. Such hunting is now largely banned, but commercial hunting for ivory, skins, and other products is harder to control and still threatens many species with extinction.

Deserts

More than one-fifth of the world's land surface is desert, where it hardly ever rains. There are deserts on all the continents except for Europe. There is a grandeur in the vast emptiness of these barren expanses, each with its own evocative name—Gobi, Sahara, Kalahari, Mojave.

•

The polar regions are called deserts because it is too cold to rain there. But the greatest deserts are those in the subtropics where the air is forever calm and clear. Here cloudless skies allow daytime sun to beat down in relentless heat—then temperatures plummet at night. With no vegetation to break the flow, winds whip across the desert, blowing dust and sand in every eye and drying up the land.

•

Satellite pictures show deserts as great brown and yellow scars on Earth's rich, green continents—seemingly devoid of life. Even close up, they can appear barren. Yet this lifelessness is an illusion—an astonishing variety of both plants and animals survive there, using an extraordinary range of tricks to cling to life in extreme conditions.

Where are deserts?

Great Basin

Sonoran
Desert

Sahara

Gobi

Thar Desert

Tropic of
Cancer

Equator

Atacama
Desert

Great Sandy
Desert

Tropic of
Capricorn

Namib
Desert

Great Victoria Desert

Simpson Desert

Comparing deserts

| Saguaro cactus | Barrel cactus | Buffel grass | Joshua tree | Prickly pear | Date palms | Glasswort | Acacia bush | Oleander bush |

North America
North America's deserts have vast plains and towering cliffs. The Great Basin is sagebrush scrub. To the south, Joshua trees and creosote bushes punctuate the Mojave. Farther south, giant cacti like the saguaro stand like pillars in the Sonoran.

Africa
Landscapes in the Sahara vary from rocky hamadas to seas of sand dunes (ergs). It is so hot that vast areas are barren and plants often grow only near oases, where date palms may also grow. The Namib has the world's biggest dunes—up to 1,300 ft (400 m) high.

Asia
Asia's Gobi desert is hot in summer, but in winter there are no barriers to protect it from the icy air blowing in from Siberia to the north. Vegetation blooms briefly after the spring rains and survives through the early summer before the searing heat dries it out. The dominant plants are saxaul shrubs, and patches of low plants like saltwort and feather grass.

| Saxaul bushes | Feather grass | Sagebrush | Saltwort |

Desert environments

Deserts vary hugely, but the driest deserts get less than 4 in (100 mm) of rain a year. Areas with less than about 24 in (600 mm) are said to be semi-arid. In hot deserts rain comes in short, heavy showers that run off the land quickly—or evaporate almost instantly into the warm, dry air.

°C °F Temperature   Rainfall   mm in

40 — 104
35 — 95
30 — 86
25 — 77
20 — 68
15 — 59
10 — 50

5.0 — ⅕
4.0 — ⅙
3.0 — ⅛
2.0 — ⅓₃
0 — 0

J F M A M J J A S O N D

Scorching sun
All deserts are dry. Some are very hot, too, and daytime summer temperatures can soar to 122°F (50°C), although nights are cool. This graph shows conditions for In Salah, Algeria, which is exceptionally dry.

Oasis
Little rain falls on the surface, but there is often water in the desert below ground. Some is subterranean water from beyond the desert. Some is water left over from wetter times in the ancient past. Oases occur where this underground water gets to the surface.

Desert bloom
Many desert plants and seeds may lie dormant for months or even years, apparently lifeless—then burst briefly into flower when rain comes. They often germinate and bloom within hours, then die after scattering seed.

African deserts

There are three great deserts in Africa: the Namib and Kalahari in the south, and the vast Sahara that covers almost all of northern Africa. The Sahara is not only the largest desert on Earth but it is also the hottest. It is completely waterless over vast areas, yet many creatures can survive even here—tough-skinned lizards and snakes, rodents, goats and gazelles, and countless insects.

Namib coastal desert
The great sand dunes of the southern Namib seem barren, but beetles, spiders, and even springbok antelopes survive here—and below the surface live golden moles.

Dromedary

Camels cope with desert heat by letting their blood warm up during the day then cool at night. Their fur shields them from the sun. By drinking a third of their weight in water at one go, then storing it in their stomach, they can last days without water. They draw on the fat they store in their hump for food.

Browsers and foragers
The biggest creatures in the desert by far are camels, who can survive a week without water and much longer without food. On the desert fringes, anubis and hamadryas baboons manage to find enough grass seed, roots, and bulbs to survive.

Kalahari desert
Although a desert, the sandy Kalahari has plenty of vegetation and is home to many large animals, including gemsbok antelopes, zebras, and cheetahs.

Darkling beetle

Darkling beetles are among the most numerous beetles in the Namib Desert. When the damp fog rolls in from the sea, they stand on their heads so that drops of water collect on their bodies and run down toward their mouths. Many darkling beetles are white to reflect the desert sun.

Small mammals
Medium-sized mammals find it hard to cope with desert heat, but small ones can burrow and hide in the shade. The Sahara has 40 species of rodent, including gerbils, mice, jerboas, and rock hares. There are also long-eared desert hedgehogs and rock hyraxes.

Pale chanting goshawk

This small goshawk is often seen in the Namib Desert perching on a tree—or even walking about on the ground, looking very much like a secretary bird. Indeed, it spends far more time on the ground than any other hawk—perhaps to save energy—and often runs after prey at great speed.

Insects
Their waterproof casing helps insects and spiders to live in the Sahara. There are flying insects, such as flies, wasps, and locusts; flightless insects, such as ants, termites, and beetles (e.g. scarabs); spiders, such as wolf and jumping spiders; and many scorpions.

Fat-tailed gerbil

Like many desert rodents, this gerbil escapes the heat by resting in burrows and comes out in the cool of night to feed on seeds and insect grubs. It gets its name because it stores fat in its stubby tail. When food is plentiful, the tail swells up so much that the gerbil can barely drag it along. Then, when food is scarce, the fat is used up and the tail slims down.

Birds of prey
Birds can fly long distances in search of food and water, and have higher body temperatures than mammals. Many birds can survive in the Sahara. Large birds of prey include black-faced vultures, lanner falcons, and pygmy falcons.

Sahara

The world's largest desert is a mix of hamada (rocky uplands), reg (silt and gravel), and erg (seas of sand).

MEDITERRANEAN SEA

Nile

RED SEA

Predatory mammals

Although there is little plant life for food in the desert, there are other animals to eat. There are many medium-sized predators in the Sahara, including dogs, such as hyenas, jackals, and fennec foxes, and cats, such as the caracal and sandcat.

Arabian desert

Many larger animals here have been slaughtered by motorized hunting parties, but a few addax antelopes survive and there are many rodents and lizards.

Striped hyena

Unlike their larger spotted cousins, striped hyenas are solitary animals, usually hunting alone. They live only in pairs during the breeding season. They sometimes feed on carrion, such as the remains of cat kills, but also prey on lambs, small mammals, and reptiles.

Grazing mammals

Surprisingly, many grazing animals live in the Sahara. Grevy's zebras roam the fringes, while sheep, goats, ibexes, and asses haunt mountain areas. Antelopes, such as the addax, scimitar-horned oryx, and dama, dorcas, and sand gazelles live in the heart of the desert.

Reptiles and amphibians

Reptiles are well-adapted to life in the desert. They have thick, moisture-proof skins and rely on the sun for energy. There are over 100 species in the Sahara, including lizards like the desert monitor, geckos, and skinks, as well as snakes and tortoises.

Courser

Coursers are a group of nine species of desert bird found in Africa, India, and Australia. They are strong fliers, but they are more often seen chasing the insects they catch by sprinting along the ground, or resting between bursts of running. The picture shows the cream-colored courser of Africa.

Springbok

The Namib Desert in the south of Africa has its own range of grazers. There is little rain here, yet the air is so humid from coastal fogs that mountain zebras and antelopes like the gemsbok and springbok can find enough moisture and grass to survive. The 2½ ft- (76 cm-) high springbok is known for its ability to spring up to 11½ ft (3.5 m) in the air when alarmed.

Birds of the air

In fall, birds like warblers, swallows, and martins fly south over the Sahara to escape the European winter, then fly north the following spring. Some birds, such as wheatears, even stay for the winter; others, like rock sparrows and weavers, live here all year.

Black-bellied sandgrouse

The need for water plays a key role in the life of the black-bellied sandgrouse. It roosts in small flocks on open ground, then at dawn it flies to a water hole, where several flocks may jostle for water. When it has young, it soaks its breast feathers to take water back for the chicks to drink.

Toad-headed agamid

Agamids are a huge group of lizards with chisel-shaped front teeth. The toad-headed agamid has a round head that looks rather like a toad's. Like many desert creatures, it shelters underground, digging a short tunnel, or burying itself in sand by wriggling from side to side. The picture shows it in defense mode, with its tail raised and rolled up.

Ground birds

With few trees, ground birds can cope better here than perching birds. Ostriches and guinea fowl are seen on the fringes, while houbaras and Nubian bustards live further in. Like many desert creatures, bustards get most of their water from the prey that they eat.

41

Desert survival

Life in the Sahara is life on the edge. The creatures that live here must be able to cope not only with the extreme heat and lack of water but also with the scarcity of food. Grazing animals and other herbivores often have to roam far and wide in search of plants to eat—and cope with the lean times when there is little growing anywhere. Predators, too, find prey scarce, and larger hunters can go many weeks without a kill.

Caracal
The fast-running caracal is the desert's biggest cat, hunting at dusk for reptiles, birds like sandgrouse, and mammals like the beira.

Fat sand rat
The fat sand rat is a gerbil that feeds on seeds. It copes with lean times by living off the thick layer of fat all over its body, built up when food is plentiful.

Spitting red cobra
Spitting cobras live near oases where they can find prey. They hunt at night for rodents, lizards, and small birds, which they kill with their venom-injecting fangs.

Ants
Honey pot ants stroke aphids and cochineal insects with their antennae to collect honeydew—a sugary substance that these insects secrete.

African desert food web

The small range of creatures in the desert means food webs here are much simpler than elsewhere. Moreover, while in other habitats many species may feed on a similar range of food and occupy similar places in the food web, food in the desert is so scarce that each kind of food may support only a single species. Predators like big cats and dogs cannot afford to be too choosy about their prey when times are lean.

Ant lion
Ant lions are large insects. Their larvae dig funnel-shaped pits to trap ants. They hide in the pits with only their jaws showing and flick sand to knock ants into the trap.

Pintail sandgrouse
During the day the pintail sandgrouse forages far and wide for seeds.

Desert adaptations: Walking on sand

Walking on soft, scorching hot sand is not easy, so many desert mammals have specially adapted feet. Desert cats like the sand cat, for instance, have fur pads on the underside of their feet to protect them from the heat. The hooves of the addax antelope are unusually large to stop them sinking into soft sand. Camels' feet are both large and padded.

Addax
Extra wide hooves spread the weight of the addax over a greater area.

Bactrian camel
Shaggy fur on the bactrian camel's foot protects it from snow as well as sand.

Dromedary camel
Thick fur on the camel's foot helps protect it from hot sand.

Sand cat
The sand cat looks like a large domestic cat. It hunts at night for rodents, lizards, and insects, sheltering in caves by day.

Lanner falcon
The lanner falcon often perches on dead trees at water holes looking for prey, or swoops down from heights of 1,640 ft (500 m). It often catches birds in flight, but if none are available it will eat lizards and small mammals.

Beira
The beira antelope eats grass and the leaves of bushes, such as mimosa, that grow in the stony hills.

Spring-tailed lizard
Small lizards like the spring-tailed lizard get the fluids their bodies need from feeding on insects.

Princely mastigure
Like other Uromastyx lizards of the Sahara, the princely mastigure has a spiny tail. It feeds on small mammals and eggs.

Desert lizards
Lizards are well-equipped to cope with desert conditions. They have thick skins that cut moisture loss to a minimum. The warm sun, which makes many mammals suffer, actually gives lizards (like all reptiles) the energy to hunt, though they become sluggish in the cold of night. Sometimes, the Saharan sun can be too hot even for lizards, so they move from one shadow to another.

Wildlife at risk!

Northern bald ibis
The northern bald ibis is now almost extinct, for reasons not fully understood, with less than 50 birds left in Algeria and Morocco. Its cousin, the sacred ibis, revered and mummified by the ancient Egyptians, is now extinct in Egypt and elsewhere in Africa.

Dama gazelle
Once numerous in the Sahara, tens of thousands of dama gazelles have been killed by hunters. The gazelles have also suffered because the grassy desert fringes where herds spend the drier part of the year are being stripped bare by livestock.

Desertification
In the last 50 years, the Sahara has expanded southward to cover a further 250,000 sq miles (650,000 sq km). This is partly due to climatic changes, but is also a result of the overgrazing of desert fringes by livestock, cutting down trees for firewood, and increasing extraction of groundwater for farming.

Sahara Desert

The Sahara stretches 3,100 miles (5,000 km) across Africa from the Red Sea to the Atlantic Ocean and covers 3.3 million sq miles (8.6 million sq km), an area bigger than the U.S. Most of it is an immense plain of gravel and dust (called *reg* by the Arab nomads who live there), stretching away to the horizon. In only a few places the plain is broken by rocky mountains (*hamada*) and vast seas of sand dunes (*erg*). In the heart of the desert, a year can go by without rain, and the sun beats down with such ferocity that temperatures soar to over 120°F (49°C). At night, the temperature drops, allowing many animals to come out in search of water or food. Occasionally, there are oases—lush, green islands in the desert. This is where water from underground seeps to the surface to create moist areas where palm trees and other plants grow and where animals may drink.

Dusk at the oasis

In the west, the sun sinks below the horizon in a blaze of orange and purple to bring to an end another scorching Sahara day. The temperature is already beginning to drop in areas of deep shadow, and animals that have remained hidden during the heat of the day are beginning to venture out to find food and water.

•

At the pool's edge, a weary dorcas gazelle laps water with relief after a long, hot walk. A little troop of Egyptian plovers wade into the muddy shallows, while a pair of helmeted guineafowl peck for seeds along the shore. A buzzing in the air signifies the presence of swarms of jeweled wasps and mosquitoes.

•

Near the pool, a long-eared desert hedgehog is foraging for ants while a fennec fox is just emerging from its burrow to hunt. A fringe-toed lizard scoots across a patch of sand still hot from the sun, spreading the fringe of scales on its feet to stop it from sinking into the soft sand, and holding its body high to avoid the scorching sandy surface.

•

Farther off, oryx and addax are feeding on the lush vegetation while camels, no longer hungry or thirsty, wander into the dunes.

KEY

1 Desert hedgehog
2 Domino beetles
3 Pintail sandgrouse
4 Addaxes
5 Skink
6 Dorcas gazelles
7 Egyptian plovers
8 Guineafowl
9 Gundis
10 Spiny mouse
11 Saw-scaled adder
12 Spitting spider
13 Fringe-toed lizard
14 Fennec fox
15 Scorpions
16 Oryx
17 Mosquito
18 Lappet-faced vultures
19 Dromedary camel

Asian deserts

Asia's Gobi desert is one of the world's forgotten places—a vast, parched, windswept expanse stretching across southern Mongolia into China. Unlike the ever-hot Sahara, the Gobi swings from scorching summer days—over 113°F (45°C)—to icy winters—often below -40°F (-40°C). This harshness has made it a refuge for creatures hardy enough to survive, including some of the world's rarest animals, such as the Bactrian camel.

Southern deserts
No other deserts have such scorching summers and icy winters yet many jerboas and many reptiles, such as the huge gray monitor, live here. So too does the very rare desert cheetah.

Takla Makhan
This giant high-altitude plateau is the largest sand desert in Asia.

CAUCASUS MOUNTAINS

Thar desert
The Thar is home not only to desert foxes and caracals, but also large grazers, such as chinkaras and blackbucks, plus many rodents and 141 species of bird, such as the rare great Indian bustard.

Reptiles
Many reptiles cope with the Gobi's extremes by burrowing. There are tortoises and many kinds of gecko and lizard, such as the gray monitor and Gobi racerunner. They are food for snakes like the lebetine viper and tatar sand boa.

Mongolian agama lizard

The Mongolian agama lizard is one of over 300 plump-bodied lizards called agamids. They nearly all have thin tails, long legs, and triangular heads with chisel-shaped jaws. Like other desert agamids, the Mongolian agama is a burrowing creature, and spends the cold winter asleep deep below ground.

Pallid harrier

Slender, long-winged pallid and pied harriers are birds of prey that nest on the ground or in bushes. They catch small mammals, such as jerboas, and birds and lizards by swooping low over the ground. The Gobi winter is too cold for the harriers, so they migrate to India by fall.

Gobi bear

The Gobi bear (*Ursus arctos pruinosus*) is the world's only desert bear, living in southwestern Mongolia, where the local people call it Mazaalai. It is actually a type of brown bear, like the North American grizzly, but is adapted to coping with the arid conditions of the Gobi. It is now very rare and close to extinction, with only 30 or so animals surviving.

Insects
The extremes of the Gobi make life difficult even for insects and other invertebrates. Nevertheless, there is a range of insects in the desert, including ants, beetles, bees, and earwigs; arachnids, such as scorpions and sun spiders; and woodlice and centipedes.

Funnel-web spider

Some funnel-web spiders like the brachyteles can cope with dry conditions on the edge of the desert because they live in burrows, and are active only at night. They spin funnel-shaped entrances to their burrows. Silk trip lines radiating from the entrance alert the spider to incoming prey.

Predatory mammals
The Gobi once had two big predators; the Gobi bear and the snow leopard, which used to venture down from the mountains of Tibet. These are now very rare, and the main hunting mammal is the marbled polecat, which hunts at night for lizards and small mammals.

Birds of prey
In summer, various birds of prey visit the Gobi, including spectacular golden and imperial eagles. All year-round, there are carrion-feeding vultures, such as the lammergeier and the giant Cinereous vulture (the European black), with its 10 ft- (3 m-) wingspan.

Gobi desert
Covering over 500,000 sq miles (1.3 million sq km), the Gobi is a vast expanse of dry stony river valleys—home to numerous lizards and rodents, and rare Bactrian camels.

URAL MOUNTAINS

ALTAI MOUNTAINS

Birds of the air
In summer, many birds visit the Asian deserts and surrounding dry steppes; they include wheatears, desert warblers, desert larks, and stone curlews. Other birds, such as Koslov's accentor and the saxaul sparrow, are here most of the year.

Desert lark

The desert lark lives in the warm deserts of southwestern Asia and India across to the Sahara, and builds its nest against a rock or tuft of grass. Its plumage is perfect camouflage against the sandy soil—vital in a habitat where there is little cover. A dark species lives on black sandy areas; a pale species lives on areas of white sand.

Small mammals
Small animals cope with the Gobi's extremes by hiding underground—in summer to avoid the heat of the day and in winter to avoid the cold. Many kinds of jerboa live here, such as the long-eared and Mongolian, along with various hamsters and hedgehogs.

Ground birds
The plants that spring up after winter in the central Asian deserts provide enough seed to support a range of ground birds, including bustards, such as the houbara, Henderson's groundjay, Pander's groundjay, and various sandgrouses.

Desert hedgehog
Hedgehogs cope with the desert heat by digging short burrows to shelter in during the day. At night, when the air is cool, they emerge to search for invertebrates, such as scorpions, and the eggs of ground-nesting birds. The desert hedgehog lives in the deserts of southwest Asia. The long-eared hedgehog lives in the Gobi.

Pallas's sandgrouse
Like other sandgrouse, the Pallas's male brings water for its chicks from distant water holes by wading into the water to soak its special spongelike belly feathers. In the past, very cold winters would drive Pallas's sandgrouse west into Europe in huge flocks. Now, perhaps as sandgrouse numbers have dwindled, these mass movements have ceased.

Kulan (wild donkey)
There are five kinds of wild donkey or kulan found in central and southern Asia. Also known as onagers, these are the onager, dzigetai (from Mongolia), kiang, khur (from India), and ashdari (the probably extinct Syrian ass). The dzigetai is the Gobi's kulan. Female dzigetai live in small herds with their young and a single male. Other males live in bachelor groups.

Grazing mammals
In spring, places in the Gobi turn briefly green and grazing animals move in from the surrounding steppes. Besides wild horses like the kulan and Przewalski's, there are ibexes, gazelles, such as the black-tailed dzeran and Mongolian, and antelopes, such as the saiga.

Browsers and foragers
There are no oases in the Gobi, and the Bactrian camel is the only large foraging animal able to stomach the sparse vegetation and cope with the extreme conditions. The camel is always on the move, seeking tough grass, leaves, and thin branches for food.

Bactrian camel
Bactrian camels have two humps, unlike the African dromedary, and a shaggy coat to cope with icy Gobi winters. They were tamed 4,000 years ago, and it was once thought all Bactrians in the wild were feral—that is, descendants of domesticated beasts. But in the late 1800s truly wild camels were found in central Asian deserts. This wild population is small.

Wide-open spaces

The deserts and dry steppes of central Asia are one of the few places in the world where wild horses survive. They are the only remaining wild descendants of the first horselike creatures that appeared 50 million years ago. The world was wetter then, and these horse ancestors were small forest creatures. But as the world became drier and forests shrank, so bigger horses evolved that could live on dry grassland and even in deserts, where they still survive.

Horse evolution

The horse's family tree dates back 50 million years to hyracotherium, fossils of which have been found in both North America and Europe. Since then it has grown bigger, longer-legged, longer-muzzled, developed hooves instead of toes, and changed from a browser to a grazer. But it was never a steady progression, and this illustration shows just a few major stages and branches.

Anctitherium
25–5 mya
This successful offshoot from mesohippus survived until 5 mya in China. It browsed on soft leaves in humid forests.

Miohippus
36–24 mya
With miohippus, the evolutionary path of the horse began to branch. It was slightly bigger than mesohippus.

Merychippus
17–11 mya
This was the first real grazer, with a long neck for reaching down to graze and hooflike feet for running on grass.

Hyracotherium
54–38 mya (million years ago)
Also known as the dawn horse, or eohippus, this was a forest dweller that fed on soft leaves and fruit. It was the size of a small dog, 8 in (20 cm) high, and it scampered rather than ran.

Mesohippus
40–32 mya
Mesohippus appeared as large areas of forest turned to scrub. It was bigger—2 ft (60 cm) high—and could trot and run.

Parahippus
24–17 mya
Bigger—up to 40 in (1 m) high—and faster running, this had teeth better adapted for eating grass. The move out from forests had begun.

Hipparion
15–2 mya
This was one of the many successful branches of grazing horse, long surviving in Africa.

Pliohippus
12–5 mya
An early hoofed horse, this was once thought to be the direct ancestor of the modern horse Equus.

Desert adaptation: Rodents

Few medium-sized mammals can cope with hot, dry deserts, but deserts are home to a huge variety of tiny rodents. Rodents hide away from the sun in burrows during the day. Burrows retain the moisture of the animal's breath and stay at a steady 77–95°F (25–35°C). Desert rodents get water from their food. Some rodents have huge back legs so that they can move in leaps, and barely touch the hot ground when they come out at night.

Dwarf hamsters live in burrows in sand dunes in Central Asia, emerging at night to feed.

Great jerboas are one of 11 jerboa species living in the Gobi. They can jump up to 10 ft (3 m).

Great jerboa

Dwarf hamster

Chinese hamsters are the smallest of the "ratlike" hamsters, barely 3 in (8 cm) long.

Chinese hamster

Przewalski's horse

Most "wild" horses are descendants of escaped domestic horses—Przewalski's horse is the only living truly wild horse. It was first identified in the 1880s by Russian explorer Nicolai Przewalski. There were very few and the last one was seen in the wild in 1969. Fortunately, over 1,000 survived in zoos, and in the 1990s a handful were reintroduced to the wild in Hustain Huruu in Mongolia.

Wildlife at risk!

Snow leopard
This leopard's thick coat shields it from the cold in the mountains where it lives at altitudes of up to 19,700 ft (6,000 m). But it has suffered from both hunting and the reduction of its natural prey, such as ibexes, due to human activity. There may now be as few as 5,000.

Hippidion
5 million–8,000 years ago
Hippidion was a large offshoot of pliohippus, about 55 in (1.4 m) high, that developed when early horses spread into South America from the north five million years ago.

Zebras (*Equus burchelli*)
There are three species of zebra—the Plains (*E. burchelli*), Mountain (*E. zebra*), and Grevy's (*E. grevyi*). Each arose in different parts of Africa.

Equus
4 mya–present?
The first modern horse, Equus, appeared about four million years ago. It gave rise to six species: true horses, asses, onagers, and three kinds of zebra.

Saiga antelope
With barely 330 left, the saiga antelope of Mongolia, Kalmykia and Kazakhstan is one of the world's most endangered animals. Saiga horn is used in Chinese traditional medicines along with rhino horn. As rhino hunting has been stopped, so saiga hunting has risen.

Onagers or kulans (*Equus hemionus*)
With the Asian onagers, well-adapted for life in the desert, the horse moved farthest away from its damp forest origins.

Asses (*Equus asinus*)
Asses (or donkeys) are quite similar to onagers but originated in northern Africa.

Argali
The argali is the largest living wild sheep, up to 55 in (1.4 m) high at the shoulder. Male Marco Polo argali of the Pamir range have horns 6 ft (1.8 m) long. These horns have made them the targets of illegal hunters, and the survival of the argali is now at risk.

Przewalski's horse (*Equus caballus*)
The only true horse left in the wild is Przewalski's horse. Some experts think it is the ancestor of the modern horse. Others think they both descended from a common ancestor, now extinct.

American deserts

The southwestern corner of North America is a vast area of plains and mountains, rocky outcrops and canyons, encompassing four great deserts—the Great Basin, Mojave, Sonoran, and Chihuahuan. Each of these deserts has its own distinctive range of wildlife, from the Great Basin with its sagebrush and coyotes to the Chihuahuan with its mesquite scrub and tarantulas.

Black widow spider

Black widows live in warm regions all around the world. The North American desert species is the *hesperus*. These spiders get their name because the female often kills the much smaller male during mating. The female is the U.S.'s most venomous animal, with a venom 15 times stronger than a rattlesnake's.

Grazing animals

The deserts are one of the last refuges for the bighorn sheep. It keeps cool here by keeping to the shade, sweating, and panting. Pronghorns live here too, and also white-tailed deer, which feed on huajillo brush, prickly pear cactus, and other shrubs.

Shy mule deer

The nimble, shy mule deer is related to the white-tailed deer, and migrates into the desert from forest areas in the winter. The deer move around mostly at dawn and dusk, and on moonlit nights. In the heat of the day, they bed down in cool places. Bucks prefer to bed down on rocky ridges. Does and fawns like flatter places.

Insects and spiders

The teeming insect life of the deserts includes fire ants, beetles, weevils, dragonflies, butterflies, such as the western tiger swallowtail, and the Magicada cicada (which lives 17 years, longer than almost any other insect). Spiders include many large tarantulas.

Desert kangaroo rat

Kangaroo rats are rodents that hop around like a kangaroo to keep their feet off hot ground. They dig little dens under bushes, such as hopsage and blackbrush, to shelter in during the day. At night they come out to feed and stuff food into fur-lined pouches on their cheeks.

Small mammals

As in many hot deserts, there is a wealth of small mammals. Rodents, such as kangaroo rats, wood rats, and ground squirrels, stay cool by sheltering in burrows, and get their moisture from their food. Jackrabbits stay in the shade and lose heat through their big ears.

Western diamondback rattlesnake

This snake kills more people in the U.S. than any other. Like all rattlesnakes, it has horny tailpieces, which it rattles when frightened. It eats birds, small mammals, and lizards.

Birds of prey

Most small desert creatures are safe in their burrows, but when they come to the surface they make easy targets for birds of prey, such as prairie falcons, American kestrels, hawks, turkey vultures, golden eagles, and owls, such as the great horned and burrowing owls.

Red-tailed hawk

The red-tailed hawk is the largest hawk. The female has a wingspan of 5 ft (1.5 m). Red-tailed hawks can live in a range of habitats. In summer, they are found in northern Alaska. In winter, they are often seen soaring over the southwestern desert, scanning for prey with their sharp eyes.

Ground birds

With so few trees, many birds in the deserts nest or feed on the ground, including Gambel's and California quails, roadrunners, inca and mourning doves, and the common poorwill. Turkeys and ring-necked pheasants are visitors to the more moist parts of the desert.

Greater roadrunner

The roadrunner is a large ground bird of the cuckoo family that can run at 15 mph (25 km/h). It feeds mainly on insects, rodents, and lizards, but is well known as a snake-killer. It is able to dart in and stab a snake's head, grab the snake in its beak, and thrash it on the ground.

Reptiles and amphibians

Besides lizards, the deserts are home to rattlesnakes, whip snakes, king, coral, and gopher snakes, and also the rare desert tortoise. Amphibians survive by emerging from burrows only after rains: e.g. spadefoot toads, leopard frogs, and desert slender salamanders.

Western chuckwalla

Chuckwallas are among the largest North American lizards, second only to the Gila monster and growing up to 2 ft (60 cm) long. Despite their size, they are herbivores, and they face danger by wedging themselves into cracks, breathing in three times their normal lung capacity, to ensure a tight fit.

Lizards

The many desert lizards include swift-moving zebra lizards, fearsome-looking desert horned lizards, pretty fringe-toed lizards, desert spiny lizards, banded geckos, iguanas, and whiptails. The Gila monster is the U.S.'s largest lizard, and one of two poisonous ones. The other is the Mexican beaded lizard.

Gila woodpecker

Gila woodpeckers have an intimate relationship with the saguaro cactus. They feed on saguaro fruit and peck out cavities in the cactus to get at insects and provide a hole to raise their young. But the woodpecker's cavities rarely harm the cactus, and the bird plays a major role in dispersing its seeds.

Birds of the air

Despite the lack of trees, many birds may linger in the desert, e.g. the crowned sparrow, the warbling vireo, the rock wren, thrashers, and warblers like the hermit. Birds like the cactus wren, gilded flicker, and Gila woodpecker live here all the time.

Bobcat

The bobcat may look just like a large tabby cat, but it is a fierce creature, able to kill animals as large as deer. Most of the time, however, it hunts rabbits, ground squirrels, pocket gophers, wood rats, and the occasional quail. Sometimes, bobcats raid farms for chickens and lambs—which is why many farmers hunt them. Others trap them for their pelts.

Great Basin
The Great Basin is a scrubland of sagebrush, roamed by pack rats, coyotes, and bobcats and scanned by buzzards, hawks, and owls.

Death Valley
Linking the Great Basin to the Mojave, Death Valley is the hottest, lowest place in North America—270 ft (82 m) below sea level and sometimes reaching more than 130°F (54°C) in the day.

Mojave Desert
The Mojave is a desert of Joshua trees and creosote bushes—the home of rattlesnakes, kangaroo rats, desert tortoises, cactus wrens, and Gila monsters.

Sonoran Desert
The Sonoran is where saguaro cacti grow more than 50 ft (15 m) tall. Creatures like wood rats, elf-owls, Gila woodpeckers, and hummingbirds live on the saguaro.

Chihuahuan desert
In the Chihuahuan, mesquite scrub grows higher up, and opuntia and barrel cactus lower down. Tarantulas, scorpions, and lizards lurk here. Antelope jackrabbits are also common.

GULF OF CALIFORNIA

GULF OF MEXICO

SIERRA NEVADA

Predatory mammals

Rodents, reptiles, and birds provide food for a number of cats and dogs. Cats include bobcats and pumas. Dogs include kit and gray foxes, and coyotes. Efforts are under way to reintroduce Mexican gray wolves, hunted to extinction in the wild in the 1950s.

Scorching sun

Survival in hot deserts is survival against the odds for the animals that live there. Not only is there an extreme scarcity of water to cope with, but blistering heat both directly from the sun and also radiating back off the sun-scorched ground. Facing these twin threats, desert animals have developed a range of tactics. Rodents like kangaroo rats shelter in burrows during the heat of the day and gain their water from the plants they eat. Snakes, like rattlesnakes, have venom to make a kill quickly. Some animals have large ears for losing heat; others have wide mouths. Each creature has its own way of coping with the extremes.

Living with drought and heat

Lack of water is a year-round problem in the desert, and for four or five months each year, temperatures on the desert surface are too high for any creature to survive for long. This illustration shows just some of the many ways in which desert wildlife manages to stay cool, and avoid dying of thirst.

Desert adaptation: Big ears for cooling

Desert animals have developed many techniques for losing heat. One of the most distinctive is to have large, thin ears filled with blood vessels: breezes blowing over the ears cool the blood. Black-tailed jackrabbits and kit foxes both have large ears like this.

Black-tailed jackrabbit

Blood vessels come near the surface and cool the blood over a large area in the jackrabbit's giant ears.

The blood is cooled as blood vessels come near the surface inside the cool shade of the kit fox's large ears.

Kit fox

The elf owl avoids the heat in a hole inside the saguaro cactus.

The dark plumage of the turkey vulture soaks up heat, so it urinates on its legs to keep cool, and soars up into cooler air on thermals.

Toads, like the Sonoran green stay dormant in holes until the summer rains fill water holes. Then they emerge, breed, lay their eggs, and restock on food and water for another long wait.

Antelope jackrabbits have big ears filled with blood vessels which help the rabbit cool quickly when in the shade.

Common poorwills go into a sleep called aestivation when very hot. When awake, they keep cool by gaping their beaks and fluttering their throats to evaporate water—but they must drink often to do this.

Kit foxes avoid the worst heat by curling up in burrows by day. Their paws are thickly furred to protect them from the hot ground and they have big ears to help keep them cool. They get water from their food.

Kangaroo rats shelter by day in burrows, plugging the hole to retain moisture from their breath. Chemical processes in their bodies help them turn dry seeds into water.

Many birds are only active in the relative cool of dusk and dawn. The kingbird is active all day, but always perches in shade under bushes.

Yucca moth

Yuccaboris weevil

Desert night lizard

Cactus wren

Joshua tree
The Joshua trees (yuccas) of the Mojave Desert are centers of animal activity, providing a home for many small creatures. The insects draw other animals to feed.

Scott's oriole

The noisy little Gila woodpecker is the desert's home builder, chipping out holes in the saguaro cacti and Joshua trees.

Night snake

Even lizards like Gila monsters avoid the worst of the heat—sheltering under rocks or in burrows. They also move very quickly on hot ground, holding their bodies high on stretched legs.

The burrowing owl shelters underground.

The bull snake sleeps out the day in its tunnel.

The northern grasshopper mouse makes its cool hole under a rock.

The trapdoor spider hides in a test-tube-shaped pit with a lid.

The ant lion larva digs a pit to trap prey.

Sonoran green toad in its hole.

Wildlife at risk!

Lesser longnose bat
In the last 40 years, the lesser longnose bat (Sanborn's) has vanished from many of its old roosts, which have been vandalized. This bat pollinates and disperses seeds for many cacti, including the saguaro, so the loss of the bat could spell disaster for the saguaro.

Masked bobwhite quail
When cattle devoured the grass on the edges of the Sonoran Desert during a drought in 1892, the habitat of the masked bobwhite vanished and the bird was thought extinct. In 1964, a few were found in Mexico. It is now hoped to reestablish them in Arizona.

Mesquite bush and cattle
Once huge areas of the dry North American southwest were covered in grass. But the grass is fragile, and overgrazing by cattle can destroy it, with the soil drying out and hardening as a result. Soon, the land is colonized by tough, deep-rooted mesquite bushes. Animals that depend on the grass suffer a complete loss of habitat.

Temperate woodlands

In winter, many temperate woodlands are gaunt and cold.
Deciduous trees lose their leaves to economize on the
water that is hard to draw from the bitterly cold ground.
Icy winds whip through bare branches, and snow may
blanket the ground, leaving the wood apparently lifeless.

•

Yet come spring, the warmth of the sun starts to spread
through the ground, leaf buds appear on the trees, and
delicate flowers burst into bloom on the woodland floor.
By summer, the trees are lush and green, and the
woodland teems with life. Not all temperate woods are
deciduous. Where winters are cool rather than cold—in
California, around the Mediterranean, and in Australia—
trees are broad-leaved (not conifers) but also evergreen. Yet
even here the change from winter to summer is marked.

•

For creatures that dwell in temperate woods, survival
means coping with the dramatic changing of the seasons—
or, like many birds, leaving for the winter. Nevertheless,
an amazing variety of animals do cope. Temperate woods
may not have as many animal species as tropical forests,
but they are among the richest of all animal habitats.

Where are temperate woodlands?

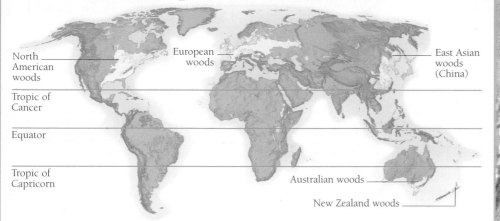

North American woods

European woods

East Asian woods (China)

Tropic of Cancer

Equator

Tropic of Capricorn

Australian woods

New Zealand woods

Comparing temperate woodlands

| Undergrowth of sassafras | Shagbark hickory | Beech | Basswood | Ash | Birch | Oak | Undergrowth of ferns, bramble |

North America
In the woods of eastern North America, trees, such as oak, beech, basswood, and hickory, spread their canopies over an undergrowth of shrubs, such as sassafras. Farther north, pine and redwood forests grow.

Eurasia
European woods vary locally, from beech woods on lime soils to oaks and birches on clay. A mixed wood may have oak, ash, and birch, with an undergrowth of thorn and bramble. Farther east, linden trees dominate.

| Fir | Bamboo | Maiden-hair tree | Dawn redwood | Rhododendron, azalea bushes | Eucalyptus trees | Southern beech | Undergrowth of ferns |

China
8,000 years ago, central China was completely covered by forests of broad-leaved trees. Now these have been cleared for farms, and only pockets of woodland are left. In these grow oak and ash, as well as maidenhair and dawn redwood trees unique to China, along with dense clumps of rhododendron and azalea.

Australia
Beyond farmland on the narrow coastal plain of southeast Australia grow dense woods of gum trees (eucalyptus), mingled with dry heaths. Farther south and higher up where it is cooler and very wet—especially in Tasmania—trees change to evergreen broad-leaved southern and black beech, along with mountain ash.

Temperate woodland environments

Although not as wet as tropical forests, water is slow to evaporate in temperate woodland and there is always enough rain for trees to thrive—typically 30–60 in (760–1,500 mm) a year. In places like southeast Australia, rainfall is so high the woods are called "temperate rain forests."

Sun and rain
In a typical temperate wood, such as New England, summers are warm, but winters chilly, with ground temperatures under 5°C (41°F). Frequent frosts makes it difficult for most trees to draw up water.

Woodlands in spring
In springtime, various flowers, including primroses, wood anemones, and bluebells, have a brief chance to spread across the woodland floor and bloom before the dense summer canopy of leaves closes in over them shrouding them from the sun.

Woodlands in winter
In winter, deciduous woodlands are transformed. The trees are completely bare and the wood is open to the sky. But the air is cold, and food is hard for animals to find, so only the hardiest creatures stay around.

Eurasian temperate woodlands

The supply of food in temperate woods is too seasonal for many large animals to live here. But there are many birds and small mammals—and an even greater abundance of insects and other small invertebrates. Each kind of woodland—beech, oak, mixed, pine, evergreen—attracts its own species. For example, some birds, such as redpolls, favor birch woods, while chaffinches prefer beech woods.

Rodents and small mammals
Leaves, fruit, nuts, and seeds provide a variety of food for many small mammals, and for insects which, in turn, are food for mammals. A ¼ sq mile (0.65 sq km) of woodland can support more than 5,000 mice and voles, plus many shrews, moles, hedgehogs, and squirrels.

Ground birds
The woodland floor is rich in both seeds and invertebrate life, especially in summer, providing an abundant larder for birds, such as nightingales, pheasants, and woodcocks, which wade through leaf litter probing for worms.

Ladybug
Ladybugs are brightly colored beetles that feed on tiny leaf-eating insects called aphids—which is why gardeners value them. Their bold, red color warns birds and other predators that they taste nasty. In fall, they gather to hibernate under bark or leaves.

Fat dormouse
The fat or edible dormouse has a bushy tail like a squirrel's. It even sits up to eat like a squirrel, but keeps its tail laid flat. During summer days, it sleeps in its nest high in tree branches, and comes down only to forage for nuts, seeds, and berries in the darkness. In winter, it hibernates in tree hollows or even in buildings.

Nightingale
Many birds are fine singers, but the nightingale is perhaps the most impressive. Often heard at dead of night in spring, its song is rich, varied, and loud. The nightingale is a shy bird, hiding in dense bramble undergrowth and darting out occasionally to feed on ground-living insects, such as beetles and ants.

Invertebrates
In spring, there is an explosion of invertebrate life in the wood, thriving on the new growth. The leaf litter teems with creatures, such as wood ants, centipedes, slugs, and snails, while leaves sustain beetles, may bugs, and crickets. Flies prey on other animals.

Birds of the air
The profusion of insect life in the woodland spring draws a host of songbirds—warblers, flycatchers, chiffchaffs, and thrushes. The rich summer crop of berries, seeds, and nuts provides food for birds, such as tits, jays, and chaffinches.

Gray wolf
The gray wolf is the largest of the dog family. Like most wolves, they live in packs made up from a pair of mature adults with a few generations of young. By working together when they hunt, they can bring down deer and other animals several times their own size.

Great spotted woodpecker
Like all woodpeckers, the great spotted clings to tree trunks with its strong feet and uses its long bill to drill for insects. Insects are its main food, but it also eats fruit, berries, and even nestlings of other birds. In spring, it can often be heard drumming rapidly on trees to mark out its territory.

Predatory mammals
There is often too little prey in winter to sustain pure meat-eaters like big cats, though there are wildcats and lynxes. Most woodland predators, such as wolves, foxes, bears, and weasels, can survive on a range of foods in hard times.

Warm, dry woods
The woodlands around the Mediterranean are mostly evergreen, with trees, such as the cork oak and pistachio.

Browsers and foragers

Many woodland mammals mix their diet a little, and even carnivores, such as martens, often forage for fruits and nuts. The main foragers, however, are badgers and boars. Badgers feed mostly on earthworms, but also eat seeds, beetles, and fruit in fall.

Wild boar

The ancestors of domestic pigs, wild boars are sturdy animals that run fast and swim well. They tend to live alone or in small groups and they will eat almost anything—digging for bulbs and tubers, sometimes eating nuts and fruit, and at other times eating carrion.

Puss moth and caterpillar

Woodland moths feed mostly at night. By day, they sleep camouflaged in leaf litter, like lappet moths, or against tree bark, like oak tree moths. Each kind of wood attracts its own moths. Oak woods draw tortrix and puss moths. When threatened, puss moth caterpillars squirt out formic acid from their tails.

Butterflies and moths

The spring leaves of deciduous trees provide food for countless caterpillars, while adult moths and butterflies suck nectar from flowers. Purple hairstreaks flutter in oak treetops, emperors near willows, white admirals by honeysuckle. Fritillaries feed on violets on the ground.

Grazing mammals

Often, only clearings have enough grass for grazing, but woodlands provide deer with shelter. Deer can also feed on tree shoots and shrubs. Woodland deer include native red, fallow, and roe deer, and introduced species, such as muntjac, sika, and Chinese water deer.

Fallow deer

Fallow deer spend the night and most of the day under the trees or in thick undergrowth, emerging at dusk and dawn to graze. Fall is rutting time. Bucks (males) herd the does (females) together and rivals fight furiously with their antlers until one retires defeated. The victor takes the harem.

Pockets of woodland

Much of Europe was once covered in deciduous woods, but the soil beneath the trees is so rich that much has now been cleared for farmland. Natural woods survive only in isolated pockets.

Bialowieza

The Bialowieza on the Polish border is one of Europe's last great forests—home to wolves, bears, elk, deer, and now the European bison, or wisent, which has been reintroduced from zoos.

Birds of prey

Many woodland birds and mammals fall prey to hunting birds. With short wings for weaving through trees, small hunters like sparrowhawks hunt close to the ground, ambushing prey. Big birds like golden eagles glide over woods and swoop on prey crossing clearings. Tawny and long-eared owls hunt at night.

Buzzard

The buzzard sometimes hunts by watching from a treetop perch, but more often it soars over woodland edges scanning the ground for small mammals, dropping down swiftly on to its victim. In winter, the buzzard may feed on carrion.

57

Woodland life

Like tropical forests, temperate woods have distinct layers, although the trees are not as tall or densely packed. The top layer is the canopy formed by the crowns of trees. Here numerous herbivores—birds, small mammals, and insects—feed on leaves and fruit. Lower down is the undergrowth of brambles and thorn, where ground birds and larger mammals find cover. The woodland floor is a deep layer of litter formed by fallen leaves, which rot slowly in the cool air. Here voles and shrews dig covered runways and there is a teeming population of insects, woodlice, centipedes, and other invertebrates.

Woodland food web

Each tree in the wood is a world of its own, and each kind has its own range of creatures. A deciduous tree gives creatures both food and shelter and links them together in a living unit. Crucial to life in a tree are the countless insects and other small creatures in the crown that feed on the leaves and fruit, and form the base of the complex web of food dependency between the animals.

Peppered moth caterpillars eat the spring leaves of many deciduous trees. The adult is camouflaged by day against the lichen-covered bark.

Eurasian Badger

Badgers like to live in woods with good cover and soft, dry soil in which they can dig their setts. These huge burrow networks have a dozen or so entrances and provide a home for a male, a female or two, and cubs. Setts are passed on through the generations, and many are a century or more old. The badgers emerge at dusk to forage for earthworms, insects, plant roots, tubers, fruit, and fungi. They will even eat small mammals. In winter when food is scarce they may eat carrion.

Pheasants are opportunist feeders, and eat not only seeds and insects, but also lizards, small snakes, and small mammals, such as mice.

Wood mice eat berries, fruit, seeds, mushrooms, worms, and insects. They go into a torpid state in winter when food is scarce.

Woodland adaptations: Songbird nest and song sites

In winter and spring especially, woods are filled with the songs of blackbirds, thrushes, and warblers. All birds call to keep in touch with each other, but male songbirds like these sing to attract a female or to proclaim their territory. Each species has its own song, which often varies through the seasons. In winter, male blackbirds sing quietly to charm females, but in spring they perch on a song post (such as a high branch) and sing out loudly to announce their territory. After finding a mate, songbird pairs build a nest, each species at a different height.

Mistle Thrush
above 65 ft
(20 m)

Blackbird
up to 32 ft
(9.8 m)

| Nightingale almost on the ground | Grasshopper Warbler almost on the ground | Willow Warbler up to 2 ft (0.6 m) | Garden Warbler up to 2–3 ft (0.6–1 m) | Song Thrush up to 5 ft (1.5 m) |

Long-eared owls spend the day in the abandoned nests of birds, such as crows. At night they hunt for voles, shrews, and other small nocturnal mammals, and small birds.

Sparrowhawks are agile fliers that use the cover of trees to ambush birds varying in size from tiny blue tits to larger birds, such as common pheasants.

Blue tits relish the variety of food in the wood, eating all kinds of insects in summer, including caterpillars, and insects and seeds in winter.

Longhorn beetle larvae can damage trees as they tunnel through them, feeding on the living wood. Adult beetles feed on sap, pollen, nectar, or leaves.

Shrews are tiny creatures that scurry through tunnels in the leaf litter, searching for woodlice and beetles.

Woodlice are crustaceans (like crabs and lobsters), but have adapted to life on land and feed on rotting wood and vegetation.

Red foxes feed mainly on rabbits, hares, and small mammals like shrews and mice, but will eat almost anything—beetles, birds, frogs, and even garbage.

Pot worms are tiny white worms that play a key role in the soil by digesting dead organic matter. Up to 250,000 worms may be present in 1 sq yard (1.8 sq m) of soil.

Wildlife at risk!

European lynx
Because Europe has been almost entirely deforested over the centuries, there are few homes left for the lynx. Originally a woodland creature, it has been driven to refuges in mountains and scrub, especially in northern Greece, its last European stronghold. Now its very survival relies on a few specially protected areas.

Gray wolf
Europe's wolves have been subject to unremitting persecution through the ages, and they now survive in only a few pockets. Prejudice means that wolves are still threatened, but small groups have been reestablished in areas in France, Germany, and Norway.

Coppiced woodland
Few woods are entirely natural. Most are artificial or have been managed. Many woodlands are coppiced, which means that trees are cut back regularly to stimulate the growth of new, straight shoots. This helps some woodland birds and butterflies but harms others.

The New Forest

Southern England's New Forest is
the product of many centuries of human
intervention. Under ancient rights, local
people grazed cattle and ponies beneath
the trees. Their pigs foraged freely for acorns and
beechnuts, and many young trees were pollarded for their
wood. Now barely any primeval wildwood survives, yet
this long tradition of management has created a unique
mix of heath and wood and preserved the New Forest as
the largest tract of oak and beech wood in England—a
haven for many of the original woodland species. Of Great
Britain's 2,250 species of butterfly and moth, over half live
here. It can be bleak in the winter when the trees are bare
and the air is chill. But in summer, when the trees spread
their green leaves, all kinds of birds, insects, and small
mammals flit and scurry through
the dappled shade beneath.

Dawn in the New Forest

It is just after dawn, yet already the warm July sun is raking through the trees, evaporating the mist and creating patches of gold amid the woodland gloom. A red fox vixen plays with her cubs one last time before returning to her lair, while a pair of badgers return to their sett along their age-old foraging path.

·

Away beneath the trees, a family of red deer amble majestically through a clearing, their flanks glowing red in the sun. Closer to, a pair of New Forest ponies are out for an early nibble. Nearby a green woodpecker taps away at a tree, probing for insects, while brimstone butterflies hover over blackthorn bushes.

·

A male wood warbler sits on a branch, trembling as it belts forth its song to warn off other males. Purple emperor and hairstreak butterflies flutter this way and that among the boughs. Up above, wood pigeons and jays flap by. Below, in an old fallen tree trunk covered with fungus, woodlice and longhorn beetles carry on the destruction of the wood, while nearby a vole heads back to its daytime hiding place under leaves.

KEY

1 Gray squirrel
2 Green woodpecker
3 Goat moth
4 Silver washed fritillary
5 Wood ants
6 New Forest ponies
7 Great tit
8 Woodcock
9 Wood pigeons
10 Chaffinches
11 Speckled wood butterfly
12 Red deer
13 Badgers
14 Bank vole
15 Longhorn beetle
16 Red fox
17 Woodlice
18 Brimstone
19 Jay
20 Purple emperor
21 Wood warbler
22 Cockchafer
23 Eyed-hawkmoth caterpillar
24 Swallow
25 Hobby

North American temperate woodlands

When European settlers arrived, the eastern U.S. was covered by a vast deciduous forest, in which roamed mountain lions and wolves. Much of the forest has gone, along with the lions and wolves, but pockets survive. These are home to a host of small mammals, birds, and insects. Some are able to cope with the harsh winter, often by sleeping or varying their diet. Others arrive in spring to make the most of the summer.

Amphibians

Many frogs, toads, newts, and salamanders lay eggs in woodland streams and ponds and live as adults among the trees—oak toads in South Carolina, gray tree frogs in southern Canada, red efts (young eastern newts) in New Hampshire, and many more.

Spotted salamander

Spotted salamanders are among the most brightly colored woodland salamanders, often seen emerging from their winter burrows on wet spring nights. But there are many others, such as the yonahlossee of the Blue Ridge Mountains, ringed salamanders in the Missouri woodlands, marbled salamanders around the Great Lakes, and Jefferson salamanders in New England.

Insects, invertebrates

Spring leaves sustain an army of weevils and gall wasps, while a host of beetles feed on the wood of trees. But the thick leaf litter on the forest floor is one of the world's richest micro-habitats, teeming with small creatures, such as ants, centipedes, slugs, and snails.

Blue jay

Blue jays are very pretty and also very bold. Like other jays, they are noisy and aggressive, sometimes chasing songbirds and eating their eggs and nestlings. More often, though, blue jays feed on nuts and seeds, which they bury in fall, perhaps to provide a store of food for the harsh winter.

Birds of the air

Even in winter, the woods echo with the calls of birds like chickadees, titmice, woodpeckers, and even cardinals. In spring, squadrons of migrants—warblers, vireos, nuthatches, redstarts—wing in from the south to make the most of the feast of insects and new plant growth.

Sawfly

Sawflies, such as the oak slug, are a huge family of wasplike insects. Females have a sawlike tail for slicing into plants to lay eggs. When sawfly larvae emerge from their winter cocoons, they can wreak havoc as they chew through tree leaves, reducing them to skeletons.

Eastern box turtle

Box turtles get their name because their plastron (underside) is hinged, so they can fold up into a box shape to protect themselves from predators. The eastern box feeds on worms, slugs, mushrooms, and fruit. In hot summers, it may bury itself in muddy pools to keep cool.

Reptiles

Areas of wetland and fields in the woods of eastern North America provide prey and shelter for many reptiles, including wood turtles, skinks, and snakes, such as the garter snake, the rough green snake, and the copperhead.

Adirondack Mountains
In the valleys of the north, forests of sugar maple, birch, and pine are home to 54 species of mammal, including beavers, coyotes, moose, and pine martens as well as eagles and ospreys.

Allegheny Mountains
One of the few remaining pockets of the forests that once stretched right along the Appalachians. The Alleghenies provide a refuge for many creatures, such as bears, Indiana bats, and Allegheny wood rats.

Great Smoky Mountains
This is one of the last great stands of virgin deciduous wood, where tall and stately basswood, beech, and hickory trees grow.

Ground birds
Game birds, such as northern bobwhites, ruffed grouse, and introduced pheasants, grow large on seeds and berries pecked off the woodland floor and need to take off only for short flights. Ruffed grouse nest in aspens, where the female feeds on catkins as she incubates her eggs.

Turkey
Wild turkeys are large woodland birds that find their food on the ground, feeding on seeds and berries as well as plants, insects, and small reptiles. They are strong fliers over short distances. They were domesticated in Mexico over 1,000 years ago. Wild turkeys are now rare in the U.S., although they have been reintroduced in some places.

Birds of prey
Woodland trees provide perfect concealed perches for agile raptors that make sudden sallies to snatch birds and mammals. Cooper's hawks prey on bats, squirrels, and chipmunks. Sharp-shinned hawks grab small birds. Larger northern goshawks may pounce on hares.

Eastern screech owl
With their phenomenally acute directional hearing and their keen eyesight, owls can weave through the wood in almost pitch darkness and pinpoint prey, such as small nocturnal mammals, with deadly accuracy. Woodland owls include barn owls, great horned owls, and the fiercely territorial eastern screech owl, known for its eerie, rising and falling, whistling wail.

Black bear
The black bear is by far the largest woodland carnivore, up to 6 ft (1.8 m) long, weighing up to 660 lbs (300 kg), and easily able to kill small deer. But 95 percent of a black bear's diet is vegetation—grass in spring, fruits and berries in summer, nuts in fall. Sometimes, bears tear open old logs to get at worms, or forage for human food in cars and outbuildings.

Predatory mammals
In summer, woodland rabbits and hares are targets for both red foxes and bobcats. Gray foxes prey on insects and rodents—and climb with catlike agility. In hard times all three hunters turn to foods, such as fruit. In North Carolina woods, rare red wolves may be seen.

White-tailed deer
White-tailed deer are shy creatures. When threatened, they flash their white tails up to warn other deer and race for cover. They are so agile they can dart through tangled woods at 30 mph (50 km/h) and even swim rivers. Bucks develop antlers in their second fall and soon begin to fight over does with rival bucks.

Browsers and foragers
North America's only large deciduous woodland browser is the white-tailed deer. But because they feed on such a wide range of food—from leaves to fallen fruit—they can survive anywhere from the cold pine forests of Maine to the warm swamps of Florida.

Raccoon
Lively and bold, the raccoon has a "bandit" mask that reflects its opportunist way of life, eating anything from frogs to fruit. This woodland creature has adapted so well to human habitation that it can climb in windows, lift latches with its forepaws, and steal food from larders. If there is water handy, it always rinses its food clean— or at least rubs off the dirt.

Small mammals
In summer, there is a plentiful supply of insects and other invertebrates, fruit, and nuts in the woods for many small mammals, such as eastern chipmunks, voles, and Virginia opossums. They in turn are food for small carnivores, such as long-tailed weasels.

The woodland year

For the creatures of temperate deciduous woods, life is dominated by the seasons. No other habitat changes as much through the year, from almost arctic desolation in winter to almost tropical abundance in summer. Each creature copes in its own way, but there are four main strategies: some animals can vary their diet and lifestyle with the seasons; many birds migrate in winter; some small creatures sleep through the winter; and many insects put their development on hold until spring.

Red foxes
vary their diet, making the most of any food available.

Wild turkeys
visit the wood in winter for shelter and to feed on acorns.

Porcupines
gather in dens and come out when the weather is dry to make a short foray for bark, their winter food.

Gray squirrels
stay active all winter, relying on caches of nuts buried in fall.

Mourning cloak butterflies
spend the winter frozen alive in cracks on trees.

White-tailed deer
huddle together in areas called "deer yards" and feed on acorns.

Long-tailed weasels
turn white in winter, becoming almost invisible against the snow.

Spotted salamanders
hibernate in holes in the soil.

Winter sleep

Winter cold means animals need extra energy to function—yet food is scarce. Many small mammals survive by hibernating. So, too, do some reptiles, amphibians, and insects. Hibernation means winding down their body processes until they slip into a dormant state in which they use barely any energy. A mammal's body heat may drop below 43°F (6°C) and its heart rate to 10 beats per minute. Most hibernate in holes safe from predators. Bears do not hibernate, but doze for months in their dens.

Scarlet tanagers

Black bear

Red fox

Porcupine

Wild turkey

White-tailed deer

Ruffed grouse

Weasel

Redstarts

Groundhog

Wood frog

Spotted salamander

Winter

As the cold of winter really takes hold, warm-blooded animals can generate their own heat to avoid freezing. Cold-blooded animals must use other strategies. Insects avoid freezing by flooding their bodies with antifreeze proteins and the antifreeze fluid, glycerol. Many frogs and turtles hide in ponds under the ice. Frogs then breathe by soaking up oxygen from the water through their skin, while snapping turtles soak it up through their throat lining. Wood frogs and painted turtles actually freeze, and survive.

Snapping turtle

Spring

As spring arrives, buds appear on trees, flowers bloom, the groundhog emerges, and insects multiply. Spring azure butterflies sip on butterfly weed and monarchs lay eggs on milkweed. Birds that winter in the south, such as redstarts, vireos, tanagers, and warblers, fly in to feed on insects. Birdsong fills the air, as birds find mates and build nests.

Monarch butterfly

Woodland adaptations: Migrating birds

Most of the birds of the deciduous forest summer avoid the chill of winter by migrating south every fall. The route and destination vary between species, but most migrate between the same localities, using the stars and their own internal magnetic compasses to guide them with astonishing accuracy.

Black-and-white warbler

Scarlet tanager

Swainson's hawk

Swainson's hawk ▬▬
Others ▬

Red-eyed vireo

Black bears
play together as families and feed on huge amounts of berries in summer.

Male katydids
chirrup in the treetops to attract a mate.

White-tailed deer
switch in summer from their winter diet of acorns and twigs to green leaves and shoots. Their coats turn red.

Eastern gray squirrels
stop eating acorns in summer, and eat new growths of fungi instead.

Black bear

White-tailed deer

Eastern gray squirrel

Weasel

Wild turkey

Red fox

Chipmunk

Squirrel

Marbled salamanders
lay their eggs in dry patches in fall and guard them until they hatch in the spring rains.

Wild turkeys
head for open areas in summer and feed on berries, fruit, seeds, and insects.

Summer

In summer the trees are in full leaf. Every square yard of woodland grows 2 lb (1 kg/sq m) of plant matter. Both the plants (and the insects that feed on them) provide abundant food. All woodland animals are now at their most active. Fledgling birds begin to take to the air. Mammals born in spring grow and begin to learn how to fend for themselves.

Fall

The trees turn gold, red, yellow, and brown as they prepare for the winter drought. Songbirds flock together for the migration, taking with them the young birds born in spring. Monarch butterflies migrate, too. Animals that are staying begin to build up winter food reserves—either by eating, like deer, or by burying food "caches," as do squirrels, chipmunks, jays, and even foxes. Deer bucks seek out does and engage in mock battles with rivals.

Wildlife at risk!

Timber wolf
The timber wolf once ranged in woods from New England to the Great Lakes. It has now vanished from over 97 percent of its original range, surviving in the U.S. only in Minnesota, Michigan, and Wisconsin. With such small populations, the chances of extinction are high.

Eastern cougar
The eastern cougar is a mountain lion, native to the forests of the eastern U.S. It once roamed all over the east, but was hunted so mercilessly by settlers that it has probably been extinct for a century. Recent sightings of mountain lions in the east could be escaped pets or western cougars, not wild eastern cougars.

White-tailed deer
White-tailed deer were hunted almost to extinction in places by 1900. Then legal limits on hunting combined with deforestation reversed the decline so effectively that there are now over 15 million in North America. Deforestation replaces mature trees with bushes and shrubs so the deer can forage easily.

Asian temperate woodlands

A vast temperate forest once stretched right across the center of China through Korea and into far eastern Siberia. Most of the forest was cleared by farmers 4,000 years ago, but the remnants that survive are some of the richest and most diverse temperate forests in the world—home to a phenomenal range of plants and a host of unique animals, including the rare giant panda.

Primates
There are 18 species of monkey living in forest trees in China. Many of these, almost uniquely, live in the temperate zone, including the rare Yunnan snub-nosed, which lives high up in evergreen forests over 10,000 ft (3,000 m) up, where snow lies most of the winter.

Golden monkey
The golden, or snub-nosed, monkey has long, orange fur and blue patches over its eyes. It is mainly a leaf-eater and lives in high mountain forests where conifers grow alongside broad-leaved trees. Although it is hunted for its fur and for use in Chinese medicine, it is the destruction of its habitat that has put it in danger of extinction.

Red panda
Red pandas live in bamboo forests in the eastern Himalayas. They are sometimes classified as raccoons, sometimes with the giant panda. The name "panda" comes from the Nepalese for bamboo eater, but they also eat berries, acorns, and even insects and young birds.

Birds of the air
Many woodland birds fly far to avoid the winter cold, but eastern woods are often so mountainous that many, including babblers and laughing thrushes, need move to warmer places in the valleys only as winter sets in. Among the vast range of other woodland birds here are rosefinches, green-backed tits, sibias, minivets, woodpeckers, and crows.

Reptiles and amphibians
The diversity of China's woodland is matched by its amphibians and reptiles. 73 kinds of reptiles and 35 amphibians have been noted in one area. Reptiles include Reeves's turtles, blue krait snakes, and Amur and red-backed ratsnakes.

Oriental fire-bellied toad
Chinese amphibians include the biggest of all—the Chinese giant salamander, which measures over 4 ft (1.25 m) long, and the oriental fire-bellied toad, which lives in mountain streams in coastal areas. When threatened, the fire-bellied toad rears up and thrusts its fiery belly out, and emits a foul secretion through its skin.

Asian fairy bluebird
Fairy bluebirds are brilliantly colored birds that spend most of their time high up in the branches of evergreen coral trees. Their fluting calls and their bustling search for fruit are familiar parts of the East Asian woods.

Foraging mammals
China's most famous native animal is the giant panda, which survives now only in Sichuan, Gansu, and Shaanxi provinces, where it feeds on one type of bamboo only—unlike the more omnivorous red panda.

Small mammals
A huge range of small mammals are sustained by the fruits, nuts, and the abundance of insect life in the forests of the Far East, including mice, rats, and voles, such as the mandarin vole. These, in turn, provide prey for sables, Chinese minks, weasels, and martens.

Mole shrew
Many shrews, including the rare Selanski's, Koslov's, and Gansu shrews, burrow tunnels through the thick leaf litter on the forest floor in search of insects to eat. Like moles, mole shrews (and shrew-moles) burrow right into the soil. They have tiny molelike eyes and hidden ears.

Daba Shan
The mixed evergreen and oak forests that cloak Daba Shan are home to rare golden monkeys, leopards, and musk deer, as well as Reeves's pheasant and wild pigs.

Sichuan
Very little of the vast broad-leaved evergreen forests remain, but along the rivers black kites hunt by day and bats hunt by night. Stump-tailed macaques cling to the trees on Emei Shan mountain.

Ussuri forests
Here, on cool low coastal hills, pine grows alongside oak and walnut. This remote world is a refuge for rare Amur tigers and leopards, as well as black bears, goatlike gorals, and unique snakes like the Ussurian mamushi.

Wolong
The moist mountains of Wolong are the last refuge of the giant panda, as well as home to 46 mammal species including clouded leopards and white-lipped deer, and also 225 bird species including rare pheasants.

Korean woods
In oak and birch woods surviving in Korea, black bears, mandarin voles, and wolves roam. This is the home, too, of the white-bellied black woodpecker.

Insects

In every eastern forest, the ground and trees are teeming with ants, beetles, and many other insects. But China's glory is its butterflies, including the orange oakleaf (a perfect mimic of withered oak leaves), the Chinese gifu, common clippers, and the rare golden kaiser.

Silkworm

Many *Bombycidae* moth caterpillars make silk, but the best known is *Bombyx mori*. The *Bombyx mori* caterpillar, or silkworm, feeds on mulberry trees and has been farmed for 4,000 years for the silk it spins to create its cocoon. Originally from China, silkworms are farmed all over the world, but are now extinct in the wild.

Predatory mammals

The rich prey of the forests supported many large predators in the past: tigers, clouded leopards, wolves, and black bears. But the shrinking of the forests—and the activities of hunters who trap them for use in Chinese medicine—have put all of these animals in grave danger.

Takin

Takin live in dense bamboo and rhododendron thickets near the upper limits of the forest in some of the world's most rugged country, over 8,000 ft (2,400 m) up. They are clumsy-looking, solid animals, but move easily around the steep hills, looking for grass, young bamboo, and willow shoots to eat.

Grazers and browsers

The forests of East Asia were once so dense and so steep that the deer living here, such as sika and eld's deer, Reeves's and Fea's muntjacs, and Siberian musks, had to be small. On open slopes high up, there are bigger white-lipped deer, blue dwarf sheep, and goatlike serows.

Ground and water birds

Nine of the world's 15 crane species—including the red-crowned crane, famed for its spectacular courting dance—hunt for fish by the rivers and lakes of the East Asian forests. Here, too, live crested shelducks, mandarin ducks, and Chinese mergansers.

Copper pheasant

In among the trees of the Chinese forests strut 56 of the world's 276 species of pheasant, including some of the most splendid, such as Temminck's tragopan, monals, Reeves's pheasant, and the beautiful copper pheasant, also known as Lady Amherst's.

Amur tiger

The Amur, Siberian, or Northeast China tiger is the largest and palest of the five tiger subspecies, and the best adapted to living in cold places. Four of the five live in China, but all are endangered, with fewer than 30 Amurs left. A few Amurs survive in Korea, and their last remaining stronghold is the pine, oak, and birch forests of Sikhote-Alin in Russia's northeast, where a few hundred have been recorded. They prey mainly on elk, wild boar, and deer.

67

The lost forest

At the western edge of China, in Sichuan, the soaring Himalayas drop away into a startling landscape of high plateaus, flat basins, and deep ravines. The steep slopes are perpetually shrouded in mist, providing ample moisture for thick forests to grow. Remarkably, the special climatic conditions mean that these forests vary as much as they climb each slope as forests do from Florida to Alaska—ranging from subtropical in the valleys to alpine high up. This unique variation provides niches for the extraordinary range of animals that make western China one of the world's most special habitats.

Musk deer

The musk deer is a small animal barely 40 in (1 m) tall that lives in bamboo forests. Males have long canine teeth instead of antlers and these are used for fighting. Musk deer have been poached heavily for the scented musk oil that male deer secrete, which is used to make perfume.

Woodland adaptations: Giant panda

The very rare giant panda is built like a carnivore, and may be related to bears, but as the environment changed, it became vegetarian. It lives in bamboo forests above 4,500 ft (1,400 m) and feeds almost exclusively on bamboo shoots, which it grips in its forepaws to eat. To help it hold the stems, the panda's forepaw has developed an extra thumb pad.

In most animals, this bone is just a wrist bone, but in the panda it has grown into an extra thumb.

The panda's extra thumb allows the panda to grip bamboo firmly while eating and to snap off shoots from the plant.

Since they spend between 12 and 14 hours a day eating, pandas sit or lie on their backs to eat. This enables them to use their paws to hold the bamboo as they chew it.

Living levels

Everywhere in the world, temperatures steadily fall as hillsides rise. But two things make Sichuan particularly special. The first is the sheer range of the changing conditions. The second is that Sichuan stands at an animal crossroads, where creatures that evolved in the Oriental tropics meet those that evolved in the Palearctic—northern Eurasia and North America. Moreover, the isolation of the deep valleys has allowed some primitive cold-climate animals, such as mole shrews, to avoid competition and survive long after they have disappeared elsewhere in the world. The various forest levels ensure there is a suitable niche for this huge range of creatures. The illustration shows some of the animals that live at different levels. Some, such as lovebirds, are limited to just one level. Others roam between them.

Asiatic black bear

Giant panda

Silver pheasant

Merganser

South China tiger

Golden snub-nosed monkey

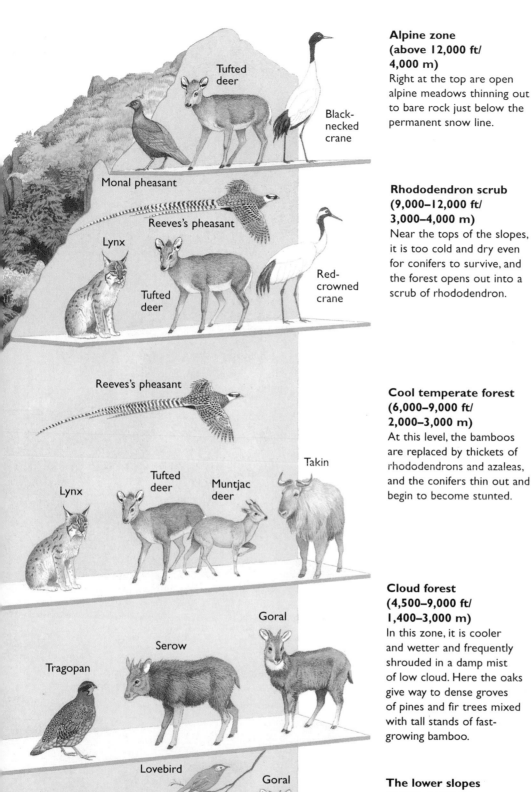

Alpine zone (above 12,000 ft/ 4,000 m)
Right at the top are open alpine meadows thinning out to bare rock just below the permanent snow line.

Tufted deer

Black-necked crane

Monal pheasant

Reeves's pheasant

Lynx

Tufted deer

Red-crowned crane

Rhododendron scrub (9,000–12,000 ft/ 3,000–4,000 m)
Near the tops of the slopes, it is too cold and dry even for conifers to survive, and the forest opens out into a scrub of rhododendron.

Reeves's pheasant

Takin

Lynx

Tufted deer

Muntjac deer

Cool temperate forest (6,000–9,000 ft/ 2,000–3,000 m)
At this level, the bamboos are replaced by thickets of rhododendrons and azaleas, and the conifers thin out and begin to become stunted.

Goral

Serow

Tragopan

Cloud forest (4,500–9,000 ft/ 1,400–3,000 m)
In this zone, it is cooler and wetter and frequently shrouded in a damp mist of low cloud. Here the oaks give way to dense groves of pines and fir trees mixed with tall stands of fast-growing bamboo.

Lovebird

Goral

Demoiselle crane

Serow

The lower slopes (2,000–4,500 ft/ 600–1,400 m)
The foothills support a mix of broad-leaved evergreen and deciduous trees, mostly oaks. Here and there are uniquely primitive trees: ginkgos and dawn redwoods.

Wildlife at risk!

Chinese alligator
The great Yangtze river and a few other rivers in China are home to the Chinese alligator. As human habitation has spread along the rivers, the alligator's survival has become increasingly threatened. There are now fewer than 500 of them left in the wild.

Giant panda
The giant panda is the best-loved of all animals in China. But its bamboo forest habitat has been destroyed by farmers and loggers, and its low reproduction rate has made it vulnerable. There are fewer than 1,000 left in the wild, and desperate measures are afoot to save them.

South China tiger
The South China tiger was hunted down by government pest controllers in the 1960s and is now the rarest of the tiger subspecies, with barely 20 left in the wild, and just 50 in captivity. Many experts think there is only a remote chance of saving it from extinction.

Australasian temperate woodlands

The far south of Australia, the island of Tasmania, and north New Zealand are so wet in places that rain forests grow, even though this is the temperate zone. Near sheltered east coasts, however, the land is warmer and drier, and here dry eucalyptus forests grow. Each area has its own range of wildlife, and isolation has made the creatures of Tasmania and New Zealand especially distinctive.

GULF OF CARPENTARIA

ARNHEM LAND

BARKLY TABLELAND

KIMBERLEY PLATEAU

GREAT SANDY DESERT

GIBSON DESERT

MACDONNELL RANGES

SIMPSON DESERT

GREAT VICTORIA DESERT

Southwest Australia
The warm, wandoo tree woods of the southwest are filled with birds, such as ringneck parrots and spinebills. They are also home to rare kangaroo-like bettongs and tiny, ferocious little mouselike phascogales. Rarest of all is the western swamp turtle.

Koala
The koala is one of Australia's best-known animals. It feeds at night and depends entirely on a particular type of gum or eucalyptus tree for its food. There was a time when its survival was threatened by the destruction of its native trees, but now the koala and many of its habitats are legally protected and koala numbers are recovering.

Insects
New Zealand has over 18,000 insect species; many are native, including thousands of kinds of beetle. But many species have been blown over by high-altitude winds from Australia, including butterflies, like the Australian painted lady.

Tuatara
Tuataras are large, strongly built reptiles. They look like lizards, but belong to a completely different group that evolved separately over 200 million years ago. The only two species live in New Zealand. Unusually for reptiles, they can vary their body temperature to cope with cold conditions. They are also very long-lived—some are over 100 years old.

Tree-browsing mammals
In among the branches of the gum trees in the hillier areas of southern Australia and Tasmania clamber and jump many agile browsing marsupials including phalangers, brush-tailed possums, and greater gliders, which can glide 330 ft (100 m) between trees.

Blue-black spider wasp
The name "spider wasp" refers to any wasp that hunts spiders to feed its young, using its sting to subdue its prey quickly. There are 4,200 species around the world, and most are blue-black in color. However, New Zealand's spider wasp is colored gold.

Reptiles and amphibians
New Zealand's frogs belong to a primitive group called *Leiopelma*, and have changed little in 70 million years. Eastern snake-necked turtles, oak skinks, tiger snakes, marbled geckos, and eastern brown snakes slither along the forest floor in southeast Australia.

Birds of the air

In gum tree forests, honey-eaters, which feed on insects in tree bark, are the equivalent of northern songbirds. Other birds include tiny jewel-like pardalotes, dusky robins, masked plovers, black cockatoos, and black jays.

Crimson rosella

Crimson rosellas are one of the region's many parrot species. They live mainly in the gum tree forests in southeast Australia, but escaped pets have colonized parks around Wellington, New Zealand. Green rosellas live in Tasmania. Swift parrots migrate between the two, breeding in Tasmania then returning to the mainland for winter.

Grasshoppers

New Zealand has no native mice, so their niche in the forest habitat is taken by large grasshopper-like insects called weta, and by grasshoppers, which are common in the mountain forests of South Island. Mountain grasshoppers can grow to 1¼ in (3 cm).

Weta

The word "weta" comes from *wetapunga*, a Maori name for the giant weta which means "god of ugly things." There are over 100 species of weta in New Zealand, besides the giant. Tree wetas spend the day in tree holes, with their spiked back legs sticking out. Ground wetas live in tunnels dug in the soil.

Southeast Australia

In among the scribbly gum and stringy-bark trees live extraordinary birds, such as lyrebirds and kookaburras, and many kinds of marsupial, such as koalas, quolls, bandicoots, and wombats.

Darling

Murray

Tasmania

Cut off from the rest of Australia, this is home to unique creatures, such as Tasmanian devils and thornbills, and rare creatures, such as pygmy possums and duckbilled platypuses.

Ground browsing mammals

In New Zealand, the only browsing mammals are introduced species, such as deer and chamois. But in Tasmania and southeast Australia, marsupials, including kangaroos, wallabies, and potoroos, hop around drier woodland floors.

Potoroo

Potoroos look more like giant mice than kangaroos, but they are part of the kangaroo family and bound along on their strong hind legs. Their favorite food is underground fungi, which they dig up with their forepaws, but they also eat seeds, roots, bulbs, and insects. Occasionally, they venture into gardens at night and dig up seedlings to search for fungi and insects.

NEW ZEALAND

South Island

Woods here are filled with birds, such as bellbirds, tuis, the Okarito kiwi, and the tiny rifleman.

North Island

In among soaring kauri trees live rare kokako birds, kiwis, and kakapo and kaka parrots.

Kookaburra

Famous for their raucous cry, laughing kookaburras live in the bushlands of eastern Australia. They are the largest member of the kingfisher family, but they prey on lizards, snakes, small mammals, and frogs rather than fish, often beating their victims against a rock to kill them.

Predatory mammals

New Zealand's only predators are introduced cats, dogs, and stoats. Since wolflike thylacines were wiped out in the 1930s, Tasmania has had a handful of small marsupial hunters, such as bandicoots, quolls, and devils.

Tasmanian devil

Spine-chilling screeches, black fur, and a fierce look earned this puppy-sized creature its name. Its jaws are so powerful, it can crush bone, and it eats its prey whole—bones, fur, and all. Yet it is not a hunter; it is a scavenger that feeds on the carcasses of birds, wombats, and sheep.

Birds of prey

New Zealand has very few birds of prey, apart from the karearea falcon, but introduced ravens take nestlings. The open gum tree forests of southern Australia and Tasmania, however, provide good hunting for wedge-tailed eagles, whistling kites, and other raptors.

Superb lyrebird

The superb lyrebird is one of the two kinds of lyrebird that live in the gum tree forests. It feeds mainly on insects on the ground. When courting, males fan out their beautiful tails, which resemble a harplike instrument called a lyre. They then make an amazing array of sounds, accurately mimicking anything from other birdsongs to the whine of a chainsaw.

Ground birds

The absence of predators has meant that many New Zealand birds, including the brown kiwi, kakapo parrots, takahes, saddlebacks, and stitchbirds, have lost the power of flight. Most ground birds in Tasmania, such as pheasants, are introduced, as they could not fly there themselves.

Safe on the ground

The two most remarkable features of New Zealand's wildlife are its lack of native mammals, apart from two bat species, and its abundance of flightless birds, such as kiwis and kakapos. There were no mammals because the islands of New Zealand broke away from the rest of the world's continents and became isolated 190 million years ago—long before mammals really developed elsewhere. Without mammals to prey on them, New Zealand birds had much less need to fly—and so flightless birds either survived or evolved there. New Zealand remained a safe haven for flightless birds until humans arrived bringing predatory animals, such as cats. Now most of these birds are extinct or endangered.

Flightless birds

Each of the southern continents has its own large flightless bird—the South American rhea, the African ostrich, the Asian cassowary, the Australian emu, and the New Zealand kiwi, along with its now extinct giant moa. These birds, called ratites, are probably similar because they all descended from a flightless bird that evolved when the continents were joined together 100 million years ago. But some experts believe that the New Zealand birds are unique and lost the power of flight only after the islands became isolated.

Elephant bird (extinct)

Ostrich

Rhea

Dodo (extinct)

Big eggs
The heaviest bird that ever lived was the elephant bird or *Aepyornis maximus* of Madagascar. This giant flightless bird, which survived on the island until humans arrived, was 9 ft (2.7 m) tall and weighed 1,000 lbs (450 kg). Its fossilized eggs are huge.

Elephant bird egg

Ostrich egg

Hen egg

Woodland streams: Duckbilled platypus

Like New Zealand, Australia's isolation has endowed it with unique creatures, such as the duckbilled platypus with its ducklike beak, webbed feet, and beaver-like tail. Along with the echidna, the platypus is the only monotreme, or egg-laying mammal. Monotremes were probably the first ever mammals and survived in Australia in isolation long after mammals that give birth to fully developed babies took over elsewhere.

The platypus's ducklike bill is used to probe the mud on riverbeds for insect grubs and crustaceans.

The platypus's front feet are completely webbed.

Platypuses lay their eggs in a long burrow dug in riverbanks.

Gondwanaland

The world's continents are not fixed in one place but drifting slowly around the world. 100 million years ago, at a time when dinosaurs ruled the Earth and birds were just beginning to evolve, all the southern continents were joined in a huge landmass scientists call "Gondwanaland."

Gondwanaland breaking up about 60 million years ago.

Confucius bird

The earliest bird with a beak, dating back 130 million years, is *Confuciusornis*, fossils of which were found in Liaoning, China.

New Zealand's flightless birds

Until humans arrived, New Zealand had flightless moas, such as *Dinornis maximus*, which grew to 15 ft (4.5 m) tall, and the smaller *Emeus crassus*. The modern kiwi is the last surviving moa. New Zealand also has other, unrelated, flightless birds including the kakapo—the world's only flightless parrot—the weka, and the takahe.

Cassowary

Emu

Giant Moa
Dinornis maximus
(extinct)

Moa
Emeus crassus
(extinct)

Kakapo

Weka   Takahe   Kiwi

Koala

Among Australia's many unique creatures is the koala. Although it is sometimes called a koala bear, it is not even closely related to bears. In fact, it is a marsupial and female koalas have a pouch. Although this opens downward, young koalas never seem to fall out, even though koalas are climbing animals and the mother clambers around trees energetically. Koalas feed entirely on the leaves of gum trees (eucalyptus), sleeping by day and feeding at night. They get all their water from their food, so never need to come down from the branches.

Wildlife at risk!

Kakapo

New Zealand's flightless kakapo is the world's largest parrot, as big as a chicken—and the most endangered. Fewer than 100 survive, and all have been moved to offshore islands to save them from cats and dogs from which, being flightless, they cannot escape.

Eastern quoll

The eastern quoll is a lithe night hunter, like a small cat, and preys on lizards, small birds, and mammals. It has suffered greatly from the arrival of cats and dogs in Australia. It was last seen on mainland Australia in the 1960s, and now survives only in Tasmania.

Giant weta

New Zealand's giant weta is a huge insect that grows nearly 4 in (10 cm) long and weigh 2.5 oz (70 gms). The introduction of rats and stoats to the mainland has driven the giant and other wetas almost to extinction. They now survive only on mountains or offshore islands.

Temperate grasslands

Wide, open, natural grasslands once stretched far across the interiors of North America and Asia. Here, well away from coasts and their moisture-laden winds, it is too dry for trees to grow, yet there is enough rain and snow to nourish a rich growth of grass each spring. Vast tracts have been taken over for farming, but a great deal of the natural habitat remains.

•

From a distance, grassland can appear to be a monotonous, bleak place for animals to live. Even on calm summer days, a breeze usually ripples through the grasses; in winter, when snow falls, blizzards can roar unhindered across the plains.

•

But grass has hidden advantages. While most plants grow from their tips, grass grows from near the ground, so it can be grazed with minimal damage. Grazing animals, which cope with the lack of shelter by gathering in huge herds, find plentiful food. Grass puts down deep roots, too, softening the soil and making it perfect for burrowing creatures. So, while the surface is placid, there may be a hive of·activity underground as little creatures sleep, eat, and dig.

Where are temperate grasslands?

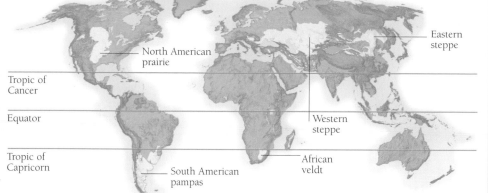

- North American prairie
- Eastern steppe
- Tropic of Cancer
- Equator
- Western steppe
- Tropic of Capricorn
- African veldt
- South American pampas

Comparing temperate grasslands

Short grasses, such as buffalo and blue grama, on drier sites | Medium grasses, such as June and western wheat | Tall grasses, such as Indian and big blue, on wetter sites

Wooded steppe with birch, wild apples on wetter sites | Laburnums, dwarf almonds on less dry sites | Steppe with flowers and grasses like sedge and crested hair

North American prairies

Hundreds of kinds of grass grow in the prairies, and as rainfall decreases to the west, so the grasses change. On the high, dry Western Plains, short grasses, such as buffalo grass and blue grama, grow. These are under 20 in (50 cm) tall, which is why it is called shortgrass prairie. Farther east is mixed grass prairie—grasses like June grass grow up to 5 ft (1.5 m) tall. In the moist east some tallgrass prairie remains, where Indian grass and big blue stem grow 10 ft (3 m) tall.

Asian steppe

The Asian steppes stretch farther across the continent than the American prairies, and so get very dry in the east. So the grasses that grow here, such as steppe feather and fescue, are short, which is why grassland with short grass may be called steppe (and grassland with tall grass, prairie). Where the ground is undulating enough to retain water, isolated trees like laburnums and dwarf almonds grow. In the moister west, clumps of wild fruit trees or birch grow, creating what is called wooded steppe.

Temperate grassland environments

Far from coasts, temperate grasslands have "continental" climates with extremes between seasons. Summers are warm and humid, with an average temperature of 64°F (18°C); winters are cool and dry, averaging 50°F (10°C). Rainfall averages 10–20 in (250–500 mm) over the year.

Rain and snow

Most rain falls in the summer from thunderclouds, but a great deal of the grassland's moisture comes from the snow that falls in winter. This acts as a reservoir to start the growing season.

Russian steppes

Like the prairies, the steppes are places of unforgettable beauty in the spring, when the snows melt and warm sun bathes the damp ground. At this time, a carpet of flowers quickly covers the ground—countless tulips turning the land vivid red; sage coloring it sky blue.

The Great Plains

Thunderstorms are frequent in late summer on the prairies, and many lone trees are scorched by lightning. But more frightening still are the tornadoes, the violent corkscrew winds that often whirl beneath them.

North American temperate grasslands

Before the Europeans came, the mid-American prairies and the Great Plains to the west were an endless sea of rippling grass, roamed by huge herds of bison. Although much of the prairie is now under farmland, especially in the east, large wild areas remain. Here, although the bison and other large animals are gone, there is an abundance of small mammals, birds, and insects.

California Central Valley is known for its blooms of California poppies. Large herbivores, such as longhorn antelopes, elks, and mule deer, live here along with small animals, such as kangaroo rats and ground squirrels.

Prairie falcon

Prairie falcons are fast-flying birds that pursue their prey across open country. They can fly low over the ground at speeds of up to 45 mph (70 km/h) before accelerating for a quick strike. Sometimes they swoop down on prey from 3,280 ft (1,000 m) up. They feed on rodents, such as prairie dogs and chipmunks, or birds, such as horned larks, mountain bluebirds, pipits, and doves.

Birds of prey
Small mammals have to come to the surface from their burrows every now and then. Once there, with no vegetation to hide in, they make easy targets for birds of prey, such as ferruginous hawks, prairie falcons, Swainson's hawks, Mississippi kites, northern harriers, and golden eagles.

Black-tailed prairie dog

Originally named *petits chiens* (little dogs) by French explorers, prairie dogs are actually rodents, and live in vast underground colonies called "townships." There were once up to five billion prairie dogs on the prairie, but the arrival of farms has cut their numbers by 98 percent.

Ground birds
With little cover in the prairies, birds must be able to fly to escape predators, so there are few ground birds, except prairie chickens and sage grouse. In the past these survived by sheer weight of numbers. Now farming has reduced them to small groups.

Small mammals
Little shelter means the prairie's small mammals are nearly all burrowers. These include cottontail and white-tailed rabbits and many other rodents, such as ground squirrels, pocket gophers, prairie voles, pocket mice, plains harvest mice, and deer mice.

Reptiles
The cold winters on high prairies limit reptiles, most of which live in burrows to avoid predators. Lizards include short-horned, sagebrush, and northern prairie. Snakes include copperheads and blue racers.

Greater prairie chicken

Prairie chickens feed on leaves, fruit, and grain, and catch grasshoppers in summer. When courting, males move into special "booming grounds," or leks. Here on spring mornings, each male puffs out his chest and inflates air sacs on his neck to make a loud booming sound. He then struts around the lek trying to outdo his rival males.

Gopher snake

The gopher snake lives in burrows and feeds on mice and gophers, small birds, and lizards. It kills its prey by squeezing it in its coils until suffocated. It mates in spring, and the female snakes lay eggs in a burrow.

Grazing mammals

70 million American bison once roamed the prairies in huge herds, but they are now almost extinct in the wild. Now the prairie grazers are the agile pronghorns and white- and black-tailed deer, which rely on speed for escape rather than bulk and numbers.

The Northern shortgrass prairie stretches from Alberta to Wyoming. It is the largest grassland in North America, home to a rich variety of animals, including mammals like white-tailed deer, cougars, and bobcats, and birds, such as ferruginous hawks, sharp-tailed grouse, and mountain plovers.

The Flint and Osage Hills are the last large area of tallgrass prairie. They were once home to vast herds of bison and elk. Greater prairie chickens are still common.

The Western shortgrass prairie stretches from Nebraska to New Mexico and is home to a wealth of butterflies, birds, and mammals, such as prairie dogs.

Predatory mammals

The bison herds that once dominated the prairies were too intimidating for even a big predator to tackle, and today prairie predators are small. Swift foxes, coyotes, and bobcats grab rodents as they emerge from burrows, but black-footed ferrets chase them right inside.

Pronghorn

Named after the prong on its horn, the pronghorn looks a little like an antelope but is the only member of its family. It is one of the fastest mammals, able to reach speeds of 40 mph (65 km/h). In winter, herds of 1,000 or more may gather for shelter. In summer, they split into smaller groups.

Harvester ant

Huge colonies of these ants burrow in the soil, and can move as much soil as earthworms. They feed on seeds and when they find a supply, they leave scent trails to guide others.

Birds of the air

In summer, many birds, including yellow warblers, American redstarts, and vesper sparrows, fly in from the south to feast on the insects and other invertebrates that appear above-ground. Others, like chickadees and eastern kingbirds, stay all year round.

Eastern meadowlark

The eastern meadowlark, which builds its nest on the ground, is well-adapted to summer on the open prairies. It walks about, flicking its tail and using its sharp beak to probe the grass for worms and other creatures. In spring, the male courts the female by showing his yellow breast and pointing his beak skyward. He defends his territory with a rich, bubbling song.

Invertebrates

The prairie soil teems with microlife—harvester ants, nematode worms, and earthworms. In summer, the surface buzzes with insects. Honeybees hum and tiger beetles scurry, while silver-spotted skippers and other butterflies flutter, and crickets and grasshoppers chirrup. In winter, bees huddle in hives, butterflies migrate or stay as pupae; other insects hide in the soil.

Western spadefoot toad

Spadefoot toads, such as the plain and the western, are easily missed because they spend much of their time underground, coming out at night to forage for insects. Their wedge-shaped hind feet act like spades to help them dig through loose soil. Unlike other toads, the spadefoot's bulging eyes have vertical, elliptical pupils.

Amphibians

The melting of the winter snow and the first spring rains leave shallow sheets of water in tallgrass and mixed-grass prairie. Here, amphibians, like the plains leopard frogs, Wyoming toads, Great Plains narrow-mouthed red toads, and black-spotted newts, can lay their eggs.

Bobcat

Bobcats are about the size of a domestic dog, and look similar to a small lynx, but with bolder markings. They live everywhere from the deserts of Mexico to the northern forests of Canada. They tend to hunt cottontail rabbits in the south and snowshoe hares in the north, but may attack deer in winter, and occasionally eat animal remains.

Prairie prey

Life is not uniformly spread across the prairies. Instead, it clusters around hot spots, such as streams and springs, isolated trees, or sheltered valleys. But the hottest spots of all are prairie dog colonies. The prairie dog is what is called a "keystone" species—a species that is central to the well-being of the other animals in the habitat—and they have done more to shape the prairie's wildlife than perhaps any other creature. More than 200 other wildlife species have been seen on or near the colonies, and many depend on the prairie dogs for their food or habitat.

Prairie dog central

A prairie dog "town" is an elaborate burrow of tunnels where thousands of animals live together. The burrows are so big that all kinds of creatures find homes within them, from deer mice to salamanders. The prairie dogs' tireless burrowing also works over the soil, so that plants grow better. Their foraging activities and droppings promote plant growth still further, so that a rich green mix of grasses and forbs (broad-leaved plants) grows up, providing a feast for grazers, such as bison. The prairie dogs are also prey for hunters, from swift foxes to hawks.

Hawks
hover over prairie dog colonies and try to catch them aboveground.

Prairie adaptations: Butterfly country

The stunning spring and summer flowers of the prairie attract a host of butterflies, including skippers, whites, satyrs, blues, sulphurs, and red admirals. Each has its favorite plants. Most caterpillars feed on greener plants, while the adults choose sweet flowers. However, some adult butterflies feed on the same plant as the caterpillar, such as monarchs, which feed on milkweed.

One of the most common butterflies on the prairie, the silver spotted skipper, sips on the flowers of knapweed, butterfly weed, and joe-pyeweed.

Buckeye butterflies usually feed only on plantain as caterpillars. As adults, they prefer aster, knapweed, and chicory.

Clouded sulfur butterflies feed on aster, morning glory, and lantana, while their caterpillars feed on senna.

Coyotes
often lie in wait at the prairie dogs' backdoor escape when a badger starts digging at the front.

Prairie dogs
feed aboveground during the day but use the burrows as a bolthole to escape predators, as a place to sleep at night, and to rear their young.

Black-footed ferrets
feed almost exclusively on prairie dogs and, being so slender, can easily slip in and drag a victim off to their own part of the burrow.

Cottontail rabbits
often live in abandoned prairie dog burrows. Both rabbits and prairie dogs eat the same plants, so if the rabbits come out during the day, the prairie dogs chase them away.

American bison

These massive grazing animals feed on wheat grass, buffalo grass, and other similar grasses. They got the name "buffalo" from French explorers who called them *les boeufs* when they saw them in herds of 100,000. Tens of millions of bison perished after the Europeans arrived, and by the mid-1800s the bison was close to extinction. Moves to protect them succeeded, and there are now 125,000 of them in small groups.

American bison
like the fresh plant growth stimulated by the prairie dogs' constant clipping of the grass. They wallow in the dust to get rid of insect pests.

Swift foxes
prey on prairie dogs if they are still out eating as night falls.

Mountain bluebirds
feed in winter on beetles and flies that live in prairie dog colonies. They hover over the burrows to spot their prey, or perch nearby.

American badgers
dig into prairie dog burrows at night to catch them sleeping. The prairie dogs have a backdoor escape route.

Mountain plovers
like to nest in the short grass created by prairie dog grazing, especially on bare soil where the prairie dogs dig.

Eastern tiger salamanders
are one of many amphibians happy to take advantage of the shelter provided by the township.

Burrowing owls
make their nests in old prairie dog burrows. When alarmed, their young make sounds like rattlesnakes.

Prairie rattlesnakes
occasionally move into prairie dog burrows. They sometimes prey on young prairie dogs, but adults gang up and chase the snakes away.

Badgers
may often take up residence once they have dug into a burrow to get at the prairie dogs.

Wildlife at risk!

Black-footed ferret
This is the most endangered mammal in North America. So reliant is it on prairie dogs for food, that the extermination of prairie dogs by farmers drove numbers down to just 18 in 1985. These 18 were captured and there are now 300. Some have been reintroduced into the wild.

Swift fox
Swift foxes get their name because they can run at 40 mph (65 km/h) and, as they are tiny (the size of a domestic cat), they appear even faster. Swift foxes took poison that was meant for prairie dogs and coyotes, and their habitat has almost vanished. As a result, they are now extinct in Canada and rare in the U.S.

Tallgrass prairie
Tallgrass prairie was once one of the beauties of North America, with grass growing "high as an elephant's eye" and with a profusion of flowers, songbirds, and insects. Now, there is little of it left, for the rich soil beneath it has been taken over by farms almost everywhere.

North American prairie

Until the late 1800s, much of northeastern Wyoming was a vast wilderness, where thundering herds of wild buffalo roamed through mixed grass prairie stretching as far as the eye could see. Today, much of the prairie has vanished to make way for cattle ranches. Yet large areas of natural prairie survive on the steep plains and rolling hills of Thunder Basin. Winters here can be harsh, with temperatures often dropping below 14°F (-10°C). But by June the air is warm again, and breezes are gentler. The grass is still fresh and green at this time of year—even the short grama and buffalo grass on the drier slopes and hilltops. Here and there, blooms of blazing stars, butterfly weeds, and Indian paintbrushes catch the eye with their vivid colors. This wild country is still home to pronghorn, elk, and mule deer, plus the much persecuted prairie dog, and birds, such as sage grouse, sharp-tailed grouse, and prairie chickens.

Early morning on the prairie

It is not long after sunrise on the prairie, and the morning dew still sparkles on the grass in hollows. On a knoll not far, a small herd of bison are munching on buffalo grass. The calves are with the females, while the young males stand farther apart. Nearby, a couple of prairie dogs stick their noses from their burrows to sniff the fresh morning air.

·

In the distance, a herd of pronghorn is bouncing swiftly through the grass, in a cloud of dust. High above, a red-tailed hawk is circling slowly, scanning the ground with its sharp eyes ready to plunge down on an unwary prairie dog. Farther off, a small flock of bobolinks are winging their way to the north, while nearby an eastern meadowlark rises from the grass, filling the air with its glorious song.

·

In the foreground grass, a pair of silver spotted skipper butterflies flit from flower to flower, gathering nectar, while a pair of 13-lined squirrels scamper by just as a jackrabbit pokes its head up. On the ground, a garter snake slithers in the grass, while a shrew enjoys an earthworm and harvester ants set out on another foraging trip.

KEY

1 Red-tailed hawk
2 Eastern meadowlark
3 Pronghorns
4 Prairie dogs
5 Gopher
6 Harvester ants
7 Tumblebug
8 Jackrabbit
9 Lubber grasshopper
10 Burrowing owl
11 Northern short-tailed shrew
12 Garter snake
13 13-lined squirrels
14 Silver spotted skipper
15 Sage grouse
16 Coyote
17 American bison
18 Horned larks
19 Bobolinks

Eurasian temperate grasslands

The steppes of Asia form a seemingly endless band of waving feather and fescue grass stretching a quarter of the way around the world. Bleaker still in winter than the prairies—especially on the high Eastern Steppe beyond the Altai mountains—they bloom profusely in summer. Countless small mammals last out the winter under the ground to make the most of the summer bounty. Many more birds and grazing animals arrive in spring.

Birds of the air
In spring, many birds wing into the steppes to feed on the spring explosion of insect life: they include crested larks, chaffinches, northern starlings, and golden orioles. Great tits and Eurasian rollers nest here all year-round.

Crested lark
There are few perches in the steppes, so the crested lark, like many grassland songbirds, must deliver its song on the wing. Its song is musical and chatty, and it often mimics other birds. It arrives in spring, and spends most of the summer on the ground, searching for insects.

Small mammals
There is little shelter on the steppes for small mammals, but a host of rodents, such as ground squirrels, jerboas, gerbils, marmots, and pikas, live in the soil. Voles, rabbits, and hares scamper through scrub and forest steppe.

European water vole
Water voles are good swimmers and dig into riverbanks if they are near a river or stream, but they often live in the steppes far from water. Grasses and other plants are their main food, and they can survive in dry conditions by burrowing into the soil.

Pallas's cat
Pallas's cat is a predator no bigger than a small dog, 2 ft (60 cm) long. It is an elusive, solitary creature that lives in caves and rock crevices, or takes over a burrow from another creature, such as a marmot. It sleeps during the day and emerges at night to hunt for birds and small mammals, such as mice and hares.

Ukrainian steppe
Here, where forest mixes with grass in the damp climate, much grassland has been lost to farming. But surviving pockets are home to a host of animals from roe deer to meadow vipers.

Foraging mammals
The steppes are one of the last strongholds of the wild boar, which forages over wide areas, digging up the ground with its nose to find bulbs and tubers. Boars live mostly in forest steppes where the food is more varied. Here, too, live Eurasian badgers.

Eurasian badger
Eurasian badgers are very distinctive creatures, with their long black-and-white-striped snouts. They live in family groups in huge burrows or sets with dozens of entrances—the record is 200. Every night, they emerge to hunt for earthworms, insects, and anything else that takes their fancy, usually following exactly the same route every time.

Predatory mammals
Wolves are less common than they once were, but many smaller predators, including pine and stone martens, and Siberian polecats, feed on the abundance of rodents. Rare snow leopards inhabit the high steppes of Central Asia.

The Kirghiz-Kazakh steppe
This is the world's largest area of dry steppe, home to steppe marmots and pikas, saiga antelopes, and corsac foxes, as well as many birds, such as pallid harriers.

CASPIAN SEA

ARAL SEA

PAMIR MOUNTAINS

Locust

Grasslands are home to thousands of kinds of Orthoptera—some predators, like crickets and katydids, others plant-eaters, like grasshoppers. The most voracious plant-eaters are grasshopper species, called locusts, that form swarms. Swarms of locusts, billions-strong, occasionally appear in the steppe and devour 100,000 tons of plant matter in a day.

Insects

For most insects, grass provides quite enough shelter from the elements, and the steppes are home to a huge range of them including ants, stag beetles, and blister beetles. The spring flowers attract thousands of species of bee and butterfly, such as swallowtails.

Pallas's snake

The abundant rodent life beneath the grass provides good hunting for Pallas's snake. Like all rat snakes, it is slow-moving and relies on ambush to capture prey. Up close, it can "see" an animal's body heat through grass. It is not poisonous and kills by constriction, but when threatened it may discharge a foul liquid from its anal gland.

Qinghai-Tibet plateau

Too cold and remote for farming, the high mountain steppe is one of the world's few large intact ecosystems. Here live large herds of grazers, such as Tibetan antelopes (chiru), Tibetan gazelles, argali sheep, and kiang horses, as well as rare predators, such as snow leopards and lynxes.

Birds of prey

So exposed are grassland rodents and reptiles on the surface that many birds of prey hunt here, including pallid harriers, imperial, white-tailed, and short-toed eagles, rough-legged hawks, and lesser kestrels. The growth of farming has made all of these rarer.

Steppe eagle

The steppe eagle is one of the biggest raptors, with a wingspan of over 30 in (80 cm). Like the golden eagle, it is a "booted" eagle, which means it has feathered legs. It is a superb flier and preys on rodents and reptiles, patiently cornering its victims by flying slowly, low over the grass.

Reptiles and amphibians

Rodent burrows are often taken over by grassland reptiles, such as vipers and the Mongolian racerunner lizard, which uses speed to escape when above ground. Briefly in spring, pools teem with frogs, such as the Asiatic grass frogs, which then go to ground in the heat of summer.

Mongolian-Manchurian steppe

The vast steppes of East Asia are one of the world's largest areas of grassland. Huge herds of Mongolian gazelle still roam here, along with birds, such as bustards and plovers. In the marshes and reedbeds breed huge flocks of Oriental white storks and demoiselle cranes.

Saiga antelope

The saiga antelope is the steppe equivalent of the prairie's pronghorn. They are fast-running grazing animals belonging to a group of animals called goat-antelopes that also includes chamois and ibex. They live mainly in small herds, but join big herds to migrate in spring.

Grazing mammals

The rare European bison is seen only on the far western steppes, while moose venture in from the north. Here and there are small herds of roe deer. Every year, winter sees a spectacular migration of herds of Mongolian gazelles down from the high plateaus of Tibet. On the high steppes in Central Asia, ibex, Tien-Shan and Karatav mountain sheep, and argali clamber over slopes.

Great bustard

The male great bustard is the world's heaviest flying bird, weighing up to 40 lb (18 kg). In the breeding season in spring, males gather at a traditional display ground to put on a display for the females—puffing out their chests, and spreading their tails and wings to reveal white feathers. The rest of the year, bustards are on the move, searching for plants to eat.

Ground birds

There are few trees to nest in on the steppes, but bustards and quails nest in the grass, where quails forage for insects and bustards browse on leaves and buds. Near water, white-naped cranes, flamingoes, curlews, white-headed ducks, and many others gather.

Taiga and tundra

Stretching right around the world in the far north of North America and Eurasia is a vast expanse of conifer forest. Known in Russian as "taiga," and scientifically as "boreal" forest, this cool, dark green forest is one of the world's largest habitats. Beyond it to the north is open, treeless "tundra" bordering the Arctic Ocean—vast, windswept expanses of grasses, mosses, bog, and stunted trees.

•

Winters are long and severe in both taiga and tundra. Snow falls thickly in fall and never melts until spring, and in the long winter night, temperatures can plunge to -48°F (-45°C). Beneath the surface, the tundra soil stays permanently frozen, even during summer.

•

Amazingly, many creatures stay in both taiga and tundra all year-round—not only bulky, thick-coated mammals like caribou, but even tiny birds like tits—relying on the shelter and sustenance provided by the evergreen conifers. In the brief summer, snows melt, days are long and the winter residents are joined by less hardy creatures, such as songbirds and insects, emerging from winter dormancy or moving up from the south.

Where is taiga and tundra?

North America boreal forest

Canadian tundra

Siberian tundra

Siberian taiga

Tropic of Cancer

Equator

Tropic of Capricorn

Comparing taiga and tundra

Ponderosa pine | Douglas fir, white spruce | Dwarf willow, hazel | Saxifrage, Arctic poppy | Grass, sedge

Spruce, fir, pine | Smaller pines, birches | Grass, sedge | Juniper, myrtle | Saxifrage, Arctic poppy

North America

In the south of the boreal forest, conifers, such as white pines, are mixed in with deciduous trees, such as sugar maples and American beech. Farther north, the forest is closely packed with evergreen conifers, such as jack pines, balsam firs, and white spruce. Unlike deciduous trees, the conifers in these northern forests have branches that slope down to shed heavy snow easily without breaking. In the far north, the trees become sparser and more stunted, opening out into grass and moss tundra where the only trees are tiny arctic willows and dwarf spruces and hazels. There are bogs and lakes everywhere in both taiga and tundra.

Eurasia

As in North America, deciduous maples, lindens, and ash grow alongside pines in the southern part of the Eurasian forest. Farther north, the deciduous trees disappear. Here winters are so cold that only a handful of tree species can survive, creating a vast, uniform expanse of conifers—mainly larch in Siberia, but also fir, spruce, and pine, occasionally interrupted by birches and willows. This is the true taiga, which covers vast areas of Siberia. Beyond the taiga to the north is the tundra where often little covers the ground but mosses and lichens that can survive without rooting in the frozen soil. In places, though, junipers, myrtles, and dwarf willows grow.

Taiga and tundra environments

The climate of the taiga is severe, and that of the tundra even more severe. There are typically up to six months of the year with average temperatures below freezing. Summers are often warm but usually short, with fewer than 50 to 100 frost-free days each year.

°C | °F | Temperature — Rainfall □ | mm | in

J F M A M J J A S O N D

Sun and rain

Average temperatures hover just above or below freezing, but while winter days can plummet below -40°F (-40°C), summer days may rise over 104°F (40°C). Most precipitation falls as snow.

Tundra in summer

As the snow melts in late spring, the tundra becomes boggy. But the ground turns vivid green with fresh moss and grass, while here and there a patchwork of tiny wildflowers, such as saxifrage and Arctic poppy, brings a brief color to the bleak landscape.

Taiga in winter

Snow is universal in winter in the taiga. The ground is frozen, too, making it hard for trees to draw up water, but the needlelike leaves of conifers lose very little water and so stay green on the tree ready for the brief summer.

Siberian forest

Much of the northeast Siberian taiga lies inside the Arctic Circle, and winter temperatures here have dipped as low as -94°F (-70°C), keeping the ground permanently frozen in places. Yet, when the long winter ends, the bright spring sun releases an eruption of pent-up life and color. Larch, fir, and pine trees sprout new shoots; mosses and lichens emerge from the snow; and tiny flowers raise their heads in bogs created as the snow melts. Animals that have lain dormant all winter wake up, and migrants arrive from the south.

Spring in the Siberian taiga

It is late in the afternoon and, although the distant hills are still a chill blue, the warm spring sun leaves a yellow glow on the ground. Nearby, a pair of red squirrels scamper up a tree, chasing each other in spirals. A black woodpecker pecks at the trunk for bark beetles and ants. Down below, a Siberian chipmunk peers warily through the undergrowth under the gaze of a hungry lynx.

•

From another tree, a flying squirrel, frightened by a goshawk, leaps into space. A Siberian tit emerges from a hole in a tree to take food from its mate to feed its chicks. Higher up, a great gray owl sits in the shadow of the tree canopy, while black-veined white butterflies, blown upward by a sudden breeze, flutter down. Lower down, near the foot of a tree, a sable, unusually out before nightfall, sniffs at the air.

•

A lone capercaillie pauses on a rock by the waterside, while a pair of brown bears frolic in the stream, swiping at fish leaping up the rapids. Farther off, a small herd of moose move silently on, pursued stealthily by a pack of wolves.

KEY

1 Siberian rubythroat	10 Capercaillie
2 Red squirrels	11 Wolves
3 Nutcrackers	12 Moose
4 Siberian chipmunk	13 Siberian tits
5 Lynx	14 Flying squirrel
6 Brown bear	15 Black-veined white butterflies
7 Salmon	16 Siberian rubythroat
8 Goldeneye	17 Great gray owl
9 Sable	18 Goshawk
	19 Black woodpecker

The Florida Everglades

Formed thousands of years ago by water flooding out of Lake Okeechobee, the Everglades is a vast marsh covering much of southern Florida. Its extent has been cut in half by a century of agricultural growth, urban sprawl, and variable water management, yet it remains a unique habitat. Not quite a marsh, nor a river, it is a winding "river of grass" over 50 miles (80 km) wide and just 6 in (15 cm) deep on average. The water always oozes by as slowly as a snail, and the hot, wet summers are as sticky as a sauna. Most of the Everglades is a wilderness of sawgrass marsh, but it is honeycombed with waterways, patches of savanna or mangrove swamp, and small islands called "hammocks" where cypress trees or pines grow tall and stately.

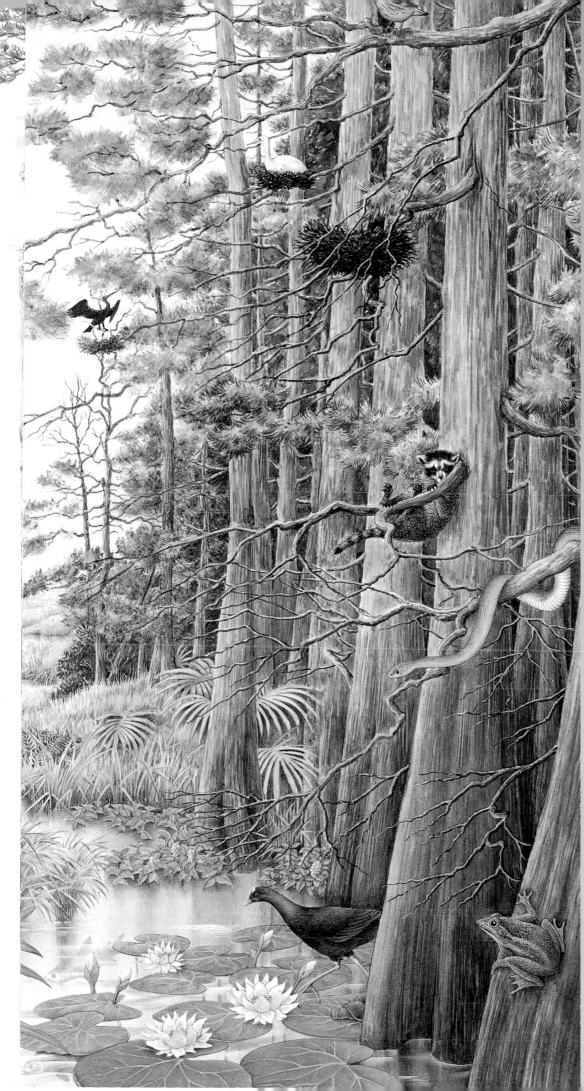

Afternoon in the Everglades

The sky has just cleared after one of the summer's regular afternoon thunderstorms, and the grass is still glistening wet. In the clump of cypress trees nearby, a purple gallinule leads her chicks out across the water, stepping daintily from lily pad to lily pad. A carpenter frog leaps out of the water to land on a thick wet root, while a rough green snake slithers around the trunk.

•

Up above, a yellow warbler launches itself from a branch while a raccoon clambers out on a limb. Higher still, a common egret settles on its nest on a lofty branch. On a far tree, an anhinga returns with a fish in its beak to its nest in bare branches poking into the sky.

•

In clear flowing waters, a tarpon fish swims lazily by, while in a nearby slough where the water is stalled by reeds, a pair of garfish and an alligator lurk. In the distance, on a pine-covered hammock, a rare Florida panther can be seen. High in the sky a bald eagle circles, searching for prey.

KEY

1 Wood storks	13 Florida leopard frog
2 Swamp rabbit	14 Tarpon
3 Florida panther	15 Purple gallinule
4 Egrets	16 Water snail
5 Anhinga	17 Carpenter frog
6 Limpkins	18 Rough green snake
7 Roseate spoonbills	19 Raccoon
8 Green anole	20 Zebra butterflies
9 Long-jawed orb spider	21 Horseflies
10 Cottonmouth moccasin snake	22 Spoonbills
11 Alligator	23 Anhinga nest
12 Spotted garfish	24 Egret nest
	25 Yellow warbler
	26 Bald eagle
	27 Everglades kite

Hippo world

Botswana's Okavango delta is one of the world's biggest swamps, a placid expanse of winding channels, papyrus-fringed lagoons, and open grasslands, stretching over 5,000 sq miles (13,000 sq km). The extent of the delta varies through the year, peaking during the rainy season and when the rains reach the River Okavango in Angola. Larger animals, such as elephants, come and go with the changing of the delta, but all year-round there is an abundance of wildlife—over 400 species of bird live here, and mammals from lions to bush babies. But the Okavango is the kingdom of one animal more than any other—the hippopotamus—and it plays a key role in the life of the swamp.

Wetland adaptations: Swamp feet

There are many places in swamps where the surface is very soft, and often consists of little more than soggy vegetation. To walk over these safely, some swamp creatures have developed big feet to spread their weight. Sitatunga and lechwe antelopes have splayed hooves to help them move over boggy ground, while the lily trotter has splayed toes for walking on lily leaves.

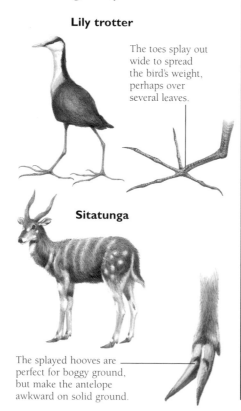

Lily trotter

The toes splay out wide to spread the bird's weight, perhaps over several leaves.

Sitatunga

The splayed hooves are perfect for boggy ground, but make the antelope awkward on solid ground.

Land clearance
Hippos climb out of the water at dusk to feed on grass. They consume up to 80–100 lb (36–45 kg) of grass a night. The paths they make through the bush, as they search for their favorite short grass, allow other animals easy access to the water. Their grazing keeps the grass trimmed, stimulating new growth and stopping shrubs and trees from taking over.

A good wallow
Hippos often deal with biting insects by wallowing in mud. The wallowing helps stir up nutrients that benefit other water creatures.

Saddlebilled storks feed on water snails, which feed on the water plants that grow richly on hippo dung.

Enriching dung
As they stand in water, hippos drop vast piles of dung that enrich the water, providing vital nutrients for both plants and micro-organisms. This benefits fish, which, in turn, provide food for larger fish, reptiles, and birds.

Born in water
Hippos are born underwater, so to reach the surface for their first breath, they must be able to swim from birth. They are naturally buoyant and often gallop gracefully along the bottom at high speed.

Huge gape
When a male hippo gives its huge yawn, it may be showing off its big canine teeth to frighten off a trespasser. Occasionally, the males fight and try to bite each other.

Hippos in water

Hippos often stay in the water with just their nostrils, eyes, and ears above the surface. They can submerge completely for half an hour by closing their nostrils and slowing their heart rate.

Hippopotamus

Hippos are huge animals, with males weighing up to 7,000 lbs (3,200 kg). They stay semi-submerged in water during the day because of their sensitive skin, and feed on grass at night. Hippos once lived across most of southern Africa but they are now confined to reserves.

Cloud bathing

Hippos spend the day resting in water to keep cool and protect their skin from the sun. On overcast days, they often leave the water to bask on the bank. Hippo sweat contains a red pigment that acts as a sunblock.

Feeding station

For hammerhead storks (hamerkops), the hippo's broad back makes the perfect feeding station, as they sift the water at dawn and dusk for fish, amphibians, insects, and crustaceans.

Feeding

Hippos feed mainly on grass, but every now and then they feed on Nile cabbage or water lettuce and so help keep the water clear. The cabbage and lettuce grows so densely over water that from a distance it can look like a lawn. As the hippos move through swamps, they break through the vegetation to create new channels or lakes.

Ground clearance

With their huge bulk, hippos have no problem trampling down patches of papyrus reeds as they climb out—and, as they do so, provide clear spaces for crocodiles to make their nests among the reeds.

113

Wildlife at risk!

Sitatunga

Because they follow paths created through the swamp by hippos, sitatungas are easy to trap, and are hunted widely both as trophies and for meat. Sitatungas are extinct in many places. Now water schemes and farming threaten to erode their refuge in the Okavango.

Pel's fishing owl

Pel's fishing owls are among the world's biggest owls and one of the few that feed on fish. Although still common in some places, they have become very scarce in others as their swamp and river habitats have been altered by drainage projects and dam building.

Black lechwe

Lechwes are medium-sized antelopes that feed on marshland plants and wade and swim well. They were once found in huge herds in wetlands in southern Africa. But their abundance made them easily hunted, and their wetland habitats are shrinking. The black lechwe lives only in the Bangweulu swamps of northern Zambia and is the subject of a major conservation project.

Mountains and polar regions

Mountains and polar regions are the world's coldest, most extreme environments. The heart of the polar regions and the highest mountains are so cold that they are permanently covered in ice and snow. They are also frequently covered in fog, or blasted by howling winds and blizzards.

•

Climbing a mountain in the tropics is a little like journeying from the Equator to the Poles. Temperatures drop 1.8°F (1°C) every 650 feet (200 m) up the mountainside, and the vegetation changes from tropical forest, through mixed temperate and boreal forest, before emerging on high alpine tundra and finally the snowy summit.

•

A few creatures, such as polar bears in the Arctic and yaks in the Himalayas, survive close to the ice-covered poles or high peaks. But most polar and mountain wildlife finds a way to live around the seasonally shifting edge of the ice—on the windswept tundra or farther down in the boreal forest.

Where are mountains and polar regions?

above 8,850 ft (2,700 m)—bare rock and snow

up to 8,850 ft (2,700 m)—grass and alpine flowers

up to 7,870 ft (2,400 m)—dwarf shrubs, such as juniper and mountain ash

up to 6,560 ft (2,000 m)—coniferous forest: e.g. spruce and larch

up to 3,280 ft (1,000 m)—mixed deciduous forest

Alps
The Alps are in the temperate zone nearer the Poles, where the permanent snow line is reached quite low, at 8,850 ft (2,700 m). Below that, vegetation descends in ever warmer zones down to mixed deciduous forest. These zones vary widely depending on how directly a slope faces the sun.

Africa
In tropical Africa, the permanent snow line is much higher. It is at about 16,400 ft (5,000 m) on east Africa's highest peaks—at 19,340 ft (5,895 m) on Mt. Kilimanjaro and 17,058 ft (5,199 m) on Mt. Kenya. Below the snow line, vegetation descends through alpine tundra to savanna. The alpine tundra is exposed to scorching sun during the day and freezing cold at night, producing plants that are unique to the region.

above 16,400 ft (5,000 m)—bare rock and snow

up to 16,400 ft (5,000 m)—Afro-Alpine plants including giant lobelia and senecio

up to 13,120 ft (4,000 m)—dwarf shrubs and tree heaths including erica arborea, erica philippia

up to 10,820 ft (3,300 m)—bamboo

up to 8,850 ft (2,700 m)—montane forest

up to 7,220 ft (2,200 m)—savanna grass and scrub

above 14,760 ft (4,500 m)—bare rock and snow

up to 14,760 ft (4,500 m) grassland with Alpine flowers

up to 12,470 ft (3,800 m)—dwarf shrubs, such as rhododendrons

up to 10,500 ft (3,200 m)—coniferous forest including cedar trees

up to 6,560 ft (2,000 m)—broad-leaved forest

up to 3,280 ft (1,000 m)—subtropical forest

Himalayas
The Himalayas are the world's highest mountains, with Mt. Everest at 29,035 ft (8, 850 m) the highest of all. Above 15,000 ft (4,572 m), all the range's peaks are covered in permanent snow. Below that the vegetation descends through alpine tundra to subtropical forest. Tibet, which lies in the Himalayas, has vast, high-altitude plateaus where it is too cold and dry for anything but short alpine grasses to grow. This region is often called mountain steppe.

Mountain and polar environments

Mountain and polar habitats have much in common. The same extreme habitat is found only on the very highest mountain summits at the Equator. In the temperate zone, it is found lower down. At the Poles, it is found at ground level.

The high peaks
Steep crags, precipitous slopes, and constant cold make it hard for any plants but lichens to gain a foothold on the very tops of mountains. Mountain peaks are arctic wastelands.

Alpine flowers
In the temperate zone, there are marked seasonal changes. In spring, snow which may have fallen all over the mountain, melts up to the snow line. Up on the high meadows just below the snow line, tiny, hardy "alpine" flowers bloom. Spring in the Arctic brings similar flowers.

Cloud forest
In the tropics, the lower mountain slopes are often wrapped in clouds. Thick "cloud forest" grows here, home to many unique plants and providing a refuge for some of the world's most endangered animals, including gorillas.

Himalayas

The Himalayas are the world's highest mountains—a vast and rugged terrain of towering peaks often more than 26,000 ft (8,000 m) high. *Himalaya* is an old Sanskrit word for "abode of snow." It is an apt name for this land of white peaks and black granite walls. But the mountains are not all ice and rock. Just below the snow line, lichens, mosses, and grasses grow, along with *Saussurea*, a low, fibrous plant that hugs the ground so closely it creates its own microclimate. Farther down, alpine flowers appear—gentians, saxifrages, and primulas—and lower still, thickets of rhododendrons turn the slopes pink in summer. Below 13,000 ft (4,000 m) blue Himalayan pine trees thrive, along with birch and juniper. Even this low, though, the Himalayas are a tough environment for animals, yet 28 mammal species, more than 120 birds and thousands of insects make these mountains their home and find a way to survive the rigors of high-altitude living.

Dawn in the Himalayas

As the sun rises over the Himalayas, snow on peaks bathed in its light turns rosy pink, while lower slopes remain in a blue gloom. In high alpine meadows, Apollo butterflies flutter in their search for alpine blooms, while high mountain voles scurry in the grass, taking a last nibble before heading off to their daytime burrows. Farther off, a flock of bar-headed geese—summer visitors from the foothills—graze on the short grass.

•

Crouching unseen on a rock, a rare snow leopard watches a family of pikas, short-eared relatives of rabbits that feed on grass. A large rodent called a Himalayan marmot sits upright listening for sounds, while nearby snowcocks peck for seeds in the grass.

•

Up above, a black vulture soars over the slopes, held up on the mountain winds, while a pair of Himalayan griffons swoop down in search of carrion. Farther off, a small herd of goatlike tahr scramble up a narrow ridge, while a markhor wanders through a gully searching for a place to drink. In the distance, Siberian ibexes leap from crag to crag.

KEY

1 Raven
2 Pseudoscorpion
3 Earwigs
4 Apollo butterfly
5 Bar-headed geese
6 High mountain voles
7 Yak
8 Markhor
9 Himayan marmot
10 Pikas
11 Snowcock
12 Tahr
13 Snow leopard
14 Siberian ibexes
15 Himalayan griffons
16 Black vulture

Polar ice

The Arctic and Antarctic are the world's most difficult habitats. For half the year, each is unimaginably cold and almost perpetually dark. But there is a brief summer when plants bloom and insects multiply and many birds fly in to make the most of the feast. A few hardy animals, like polar bears, stay all year, and there is always abundant life in the sea.

The Antarctic

Penguins
Penguins cope with the cold, snug inside waterproof feathers and layers of blubber. They cannot fly but are superb swimmers, well adapted to catching fish, the most abundant food here. There are seven Antarctic species, (e.g. Adelie, Gentoo).

Emperor
This is the world's largest penguin, up to 4 ft (1.25 m) tall. It can dive over 850 ft (250 m) to find fish and stay down for 20 minutes. It is one of the few penguins that breeds on the Antarctic ice. The female lays an egg in fall, then swims out to sea while the male keeps the egg warm on his feet through the winter. The male survives without food all winter.

Whales and seals
The Antarctic's big predators are not land mammals but seals and whales. Leopard seals prey on penguins, and toothed whales prey on seals. The abundance of fish means there are more seals here than in the Arctic, including the elephant seal—the world's biggest.

Antarctic cod
The Antarctic cod is the largest of the fish in the Southern Ocean around the Antarctic, weighing over 162 lb (70 kg). Fish could easily freeze solid in the cold polar waters, but this cod, like other fish here, has special protection in the form of antifreeze protein called glycoprotein or AFGP. This protein circulates in the fish's blood to stop ice crystals forming.

Fish
Long summer days generate lots of plankton for food, so despite the cold, the Southern Ocean teems with fish—plunder fish, ice fish, cod, and dragonfish. There are few species, but shoals are huge—and there are swarms of krill so large they can be seen by satellites.

Blue whale
Baleen whales have a comblike sieve or baleen in their mouths for straining tiny shrimplike krill from the water. Six species of baleen whale are found in Antarctica, including the southern right, the sei, and the gigantic blue whale, which is the largest creature ever—over 80 ft (24 m) long and weighing over 80 tons.

Wandering albatross
The wandering albatross is the world's largest flying bird with a wingspan of over 12 ft (3.6 m). It glides for hours on these huge wings moving barely a feather, and spends most of its life in the air, swooping down only occasionally to grab squid from the ocean's surface.

Sea birds
Penguins are Antarctica's only year-round residents, but 35 other seabird species visit in summer, including terns, petrels, gulls, and cormorants—and skuas that scavenge penguins' breeding grounds for their eggs and young.

Midge
Besides the wingless midge *Belgica antarctica*, there is one other midge in the Antarctic, and this is the only winged creature here—the midge *Parochlus steineni*. This tiny insect breeds on lakes full of aquatic mosses on the northern peninsula. Like other Antarctic insects, the midge's body contains special antifreeze proteins to stop it from freezing.

Insects
Antarctica's largest land animal is the wingless midge, only ½ in (1 cm) long. Its largest predator is a mite. There are only a few insect species, but they live in huge numbers under rocks in soil and lichens. Springtails are common around penguin colonies, feeding on plants.

The Arctic

Polar bear

These are the world's largest bears, with males often weighing over 1,300 lb (600 kg). Thick fur and a layer of blubber keep out the cold. In summer, they eat berries and small rodents. In winter, females hibernate in ice dens, but males wander over the frozen sea preying on seals when they come up to breathe. Polar bears are superb swimmers.

Predators

With so little cover in the exposed Arctic landscape, predators rely on camouflage to make attacks. In winter, Arctic foxes, ermines, and least weasels all turn white to disguise them against the snow, turning brown again in spring. Even wolves are paler in winter.

Warble fly

The Arctic warble fly, known as kumak by the Inuit people, is a parasitic fly that lays its eggs in the skin of caribous. The larvae burrow into the flesh and stay there during the cold of winter. The following summer, they burrow out again, drop to the ground, and develop into adult flies.

Insects

As lakes and bogs thaw in spring, countless insects emerge from winter dormancy. Springtails and beetles crawl over the tundra. Butterflies and bees sip on Arctic flowers. In summer, huge swarms of mosquitoes and blackflies erupt to pester animals.

Birds of the air

As spring arrives, millions of birds flock to breed in the Arctic. Wagtails and pipits catch insects on the ground. Songbirds like wheatears feed on seeds too. Sand martins snatch insects in the air. As these birds fly north, predatory merlins and falcons are on their tails.

Ptarmigan

Of the 180 or so bird species that nest in the Arctic, just a few stay all year—including ptarmigans, snow buntings, and snowy owls. Ptarmigans are chickenlike birds that can fly but usually walk slowly, eating berries and leaves. They are brown in summer but turn snowy white in winter.

Sea birds and shore birds

In summer, the fringes of the ice melt, exposing vast areas of sea. Many birds arrive to breed on the Arctic shores, including shore birds (such as dunlins, turnstones, and knots), water-fowl (such as Brent geese), and seabirds (such as puffins, jaegers, and gulls).

Arctic tern

Many of the Arctic birds migrate long distances, but none fly as far as the Arctic tern. After breeding in the Arctic when it is summer here, they head off south to the Southern Ocean, feeding as they go. By the time they arrive, summer has come to the Antarctic. Toward the end of the Antarctic summer, they fly north again to the Arctic, completing a journey of 22,000 miles (35,000 km).

Whales and seals

The Arctic winter is hard for seals and whales because the sea freezes over, stopping them coming up for air. Some migrate in winter. Seals that stay gnaw through the ice to make breathing holes, but they must keep working to keep the holes open as the ice thickens.

Harp seal

Harp seals are fast, agile swimmers that can dive deep and stay down for up to half an hour as they hunt for cod, capelin, and other fish. As the ice sheet advances or retreats, harp seals move with it, traveling in big, noisy groups. Pups are born on the ice in early spring and are then suckled for a few weeks by their mothers, before the mothers head off north to feed.

Grazing animals

Every spring, huge herds of reindeer and caribou wander north through the tundra to feed on the fresh growth, led by pregnant females. They move north each day, swimming across rivers and inlets, trekking over 600 miles (1,000 km). Calves are born en route.

Moose

Called elk in Europe, the moose is the largest of all deer, the male weighing up to 1,550 lb (700 kg) and with giant antlers over 6 ft (1.8 m) across. It is well adapted for life in the far north, with long spindly legs that move easily through deep snow and a thick coat to keep out the cold.

Mammals

Mammals range in size from tiny shrews to gigantic blue whales. They have found a way to live in almost every habitat on Earth, because they are warm-blooded or "endothermic." This means they keep their bodies at the best temperature for body processes, whatever the conditions. A puma can live anywhere from tropical forests to snowy mountains. Even so, each mammal has its own preferred habitat.

▼ Aardvark

RANGE: AFRICA, SOUTH OF THE SAHARA
HABITAT: RAIN FOREST, DRY SAVANNA
Aardvark is Afrikaans for "earth pig." In fact, an aardvark is an anteater that digs into termite and ant nests with its powerful forefeet, then sweeps up the insects with its long, sticky tongue. Its big ears help it to locate insects.

▼ Anteater, Giant

RANGE: C. AND S. AMERICA
HABITAT: FOREST, SAVANNA
Like all anteaters, the giant anteater has no teeth. Instead it has a very long snout and a 2 ft- (60 cm-) long tongue for sucking termites and ants from their nests.

▼ Ape, Barbary

RANGE: GIBRALTAR AND N. AFRICA
HABITAT: ROCKY AREAS, FOREST CLEARINGS
The Barbary ape is not actually an ape, but a monkey with no tail. It was once found over much of southwest Europe as well as Africa, but now its only European home is Gibraltar. It forages in trees and on the ground for leaves and fruit.

▲ Armadillo, Nine-banded

RANGE: TROPICAL AMERICA
HABITAT: DRY GRASSLAND
Armadillos dig for ants and spiders at night. When threatened they curl up into a ball so that only their armor-plated back is exposed.

▲ Armadillo, Pink fairy

RANGE: W. ARGENTINA
HABITAT: DRY GRASSLAND
This armadillo lifts its rear end with its tail while digging for ants.

▲ Baboon, Olive

RANGE: C. AFRICA
HABITAT: SAVANNA
The olive baboon is a large, ground-living monkey with a doglike muzzle. It eats mostly grass, fruit, and insects, but sometimes hunts small mammals.

▲ Badger, American

RANGE: S. W. CANADA TO C. MEXICO
HABITAT: OPEN GRASSLAND, ARID LAND
The American badger is a solitary hunter that digs out ground squirrels and prairie dogs at night. It can dig with amazing speed.

▼ Badger, Eurasian

RANGE: EUROPE AND ASIA
HABITAT: FOREST, GRASSLAND
The Eurasian badger lives in families in huge burrows called setts. It emerges at dusk to play and hunt for worms and also small animals, fruit, and nuts.

▼ Bandicoot, Brown

RANGE: AUSTRALIA
HABITAT: SCRUB, FOREST
Bandicoots are small marsupials that dig for insect larvae and plant roots. The brown bandicoot lives in dense scrub and eats fungi and scorpions.

▼ Bat, Common long-eared

RANGE: EUROPE AND N. ASIA
HABITAT: FOREST
This bat's huge, highly sensitive ears help it to fly in pitch dark by using sound echoes and also to locate its insect prey.

▼ Bat, Common vampire

RANGE: C. AND S. AMERICA
HABITAT: FOREST CAVES
The vampire bat lives only on blood, sucking it from its victims through its tongue. The victim loses only a small amount of blood, but the bat's bite may transmit diseases.

▶ Bat, Ghost

RANGE: AUSTRALIA
HABITAT: CAVES, OLD MINE TUNNELS
This is a large carnivorous bat that feeds on insects, frogs, birds, lizards, and small bats. It uses both ears and eyes to locate prey when hunting.

▼ Bat, Greater fruit

RANGE: SOUTHERN AND S. E. ASIA
HABITAT: FOREST
This bat has the largest wings of any bat, up to 4 ft (1.25 m) across. It roosts by day in large trees in flocks, which take to the air at night to hunt for fruit, such as bananas.

▼ Bat, Greater horseshoe

RANGE: EUROPE, ASIA, N. AFRICA
HABITAT: FOREST
Horseshoe bats get their name from the horseshoe-shaped rim on their noses which helps them amplify and direct the ultrasonic cries that they use to locate prey. The greater horseshoe is a poor flier and feeds on beetles on the ground.

▼ Bat, Spear-nosed

RANGE: TROPICAL AMERICA
HABITAT: FOREST
This bat feeds on mice, birds, and small bats, as well as the occasional insect.

▲ Bear, Black

RANGE: ASIA, NORTH AMERICA

HABITAT: FOREST

There are black bears in both America and Asia. The American black bear eats very little meat, living mostly on grasses and fruits in summer and nuts in fall. In October these bears retreat to their dens and sleep through the winter, though they do not go into true hibernation.

▲ Bear, Brown/Grizzly

RANGE: EUROPE, ASIA, NORTH AMERICA

HABITAT: FOREST, TUNDRA

The American grizzly and Kodiak bears are two of the various subspecies of brown bear, which also include the Siberian bear and the Gobi bear. They are very strong and amongst the largest of all carnivores.

◄ Bear, Polar

RANGE: ARCTIC OCEAN

HABITAT: COASTS, ICE FLOES

The polar bear is the top predator of the Arctic region. It lives mainly on fish, seabirds, caribou, seals, and other animals, but in the summer it also feeds on berries and leaves. Polar bears are excellent swimmers.

▼ Bear, Spectacled

RANGE: S. AMERICA

HABITAT: FOREST, SAVANNA, MOUNTAINS

The spectacled bear is the only South American bear. It lives mainly in forests, feeding on leaves, fruit, and roots, but also sometimes preys on deer and vicuña. It is a good climber and sleeps in a tree in a large nest made from sticks— either alone or in a family group.

▲ Bear, Sun

RANGE: S. E. ASIA

HABITAT: MOUNTAINS, LOWLAND FOREST

The sun bear is the smallest kind of bear, but it is still very strong. It gets its name from its habit of sunbathing in its treetop nest. It feeds mostly on insects and their larvae, which it exposes by tearing at tree bark with its strong claws. It also preys on jungle fowl and small rodents.

► Beaver

RANGE: NORTH AMERICA

HABITAT: RIVERS AND LAKES

Beavers are large rodents that gnaw down trees with their powerful teeth to build dams across streams and make lodges to live in during the winter. They feed on bark and twigs in winter and other plants in summer.

▲ Binturong

RANGE: S. E. ASIA

HABITAT: FOREST

This is a small carnivorous mammal related to the civet. It is the only carnivore besides the kinkajou to have a prehensile tail, which it uses as an extra limb when climbing.

► Bison, American

RANGE: N. AMERICA

HABITAT: PRAIRIE, OPEN WOODLAND

This huge, shaggy, cowlike creature can grow up to 10 ft (3 m) tall at the shoulders. It used to roam the American prairies in herds many thousands strong, and make annual migrations in search of good pasture. But mass slaughter by European settlers brought it almost to extinction. Now, about 20,000 live on reserves.

▼ Boar, Wild

RANGE: EUROPE, N. AFRICA, ASIA

HABITAT: FOREST, WOODLAND

The wild boar is the ancestor of the farmyard pig, but has bristly hair and males have tusks. It roots around woodland floors for plants and insects and also digs up bulbs and tubers. Wild boars are surprisingly fast, agile creatures and they can become quite aggressive if frightened.

▼ Bobcat

RANGE: NORTH AMERICA

HABITAT: SWAMP, FOREST

The bobcat is the most common North American wildcat. It is about twice the size of a domestic cat and feeds mainly on rabbits and hares, but also catches ground birds. It hunts by slowly stalking its victim. It gets its name from its stubby, "bobbed" tail.

▲ Bongo

RANGE: C. AFRICA

HABITAT: TROPICAL FOREST

The bongo is the largest forest antelope, growing up to 7 ft (2.1 m) tall. It hides among bushes during the day and comes out at dawn and dusk to feed on leaves, fruit, and bark. At night it grazes on grass. When a bongo runs, it tilts its head back to prevent its horns catching on branches.

▲ Buffalo, Asian water

RANGE: INDIA, S. E. ASIA

HABITAT: FOREST, WETLAND

American bison are sometimes called buffaloes, but true buffaloes live in the tropics and have thinner coats and flattened horns, which Asian water buffaloes use to defend themselves against tigers. The Asian water buffalo lives in southern Asia where it spends much of the day wallowing in muddy rivers. Most water buffalo are now domesticated.

125

▲ Dormouse, Desert

RANGE: KAZAKHSTAN

HABITAT: DESERT

Dormice get their name from the Latin *dormire*, which means "to sleep," because they hibernate for long periods. Most dormice hibernate to escape cold. The desert dormouse does it to escape heat.

► Elephant, African

RANGE: AFRICA SOUTH OF THE SAHARA

HABITAT: RAIN FOREST, SAVANNA

The African elephant is the biggest land animal, weighing up to 6 tons. It needs to eat 660 lb (300 kg) of food a day and drink more than 26 gallons (100 liters) of water. Males have tusks of up to 10 ft (3 m) long.

▼ Fox, Fennec

RANGE: N. AFRICA, S. W. ASIA

HABITAT: DESERT

The fennec fox is the smallest dog, but has the largest ears in proportion to its body. Its big ears help it to keep cool and also locate the small rodents, birds, and insects that it hunts at night. By day it shelters from the heat of the desert in small burrows. Fennec foxes are sociable animals and mate for life.

▲ Gazelle, Thomson's

RANGE: E. AFRICA

HABITAT: SAVANNA

Gazelles are graceful, fast-running antelopes with slender legs. Thomson's gazelles live in large herds in open grassland, and have to be almost constantly on the watch to avoid predators like cheetahs.

▲ Dugong

RANGE: INDIAN OCEAN, WESTERN PACIFIC

HABITAT: COASTAL WATERS

The dugong is also known as the sea cow because it feeds on sea grass, and has a long hind gut to digest grass just as cows have a rumen. Dugongs lie quietly on the seabed for most of the time, coming up occasionally for air.

► Gelada

RANGE: ETHIOPIA

HABITAT: MOUNTAINS

The gelada is a monkey that lives far away from trees. It feeds on plant material on the ground and even sleeps on bare rock. It has three areas of bare red skin which the male swells up when threatened.

▲ Echidna, Long-nosed

RANGE: NEW GUINEA

HABITAT: RAIN FOREST

Echidnas are, along with platypuses, the only egg-laying mammals, or monotremes. Female echidnas lay one to three eggs, which they incubate inside a temporary pouch until the eggs are ready to hatch. The long-nosed echidna is also known as the spiny anteater and feeds on ants and termites.

▲ Elephant, Asian

RANGE: S. ASIA

HABITAT: RAIN FOREST

The Asian elephant is smaller than the African, has smaller ears, and just one fingerlike tip to its trunk—the African has two. Asian elephants live mostly in forests, feeding mainly on grass and leaves, using their trunks to pull up plants. Most Asian elephants are domesticated.

▼ Genet, Small spotted

RANGE: S. W. EUROPE, AFRICA, S. W. ASIA

HABITAT: SAVANNA, SCRUB

Genets are small carnivores related to civets. They stalk their prey stealthily, crouching almost flat before pouncing. They catch most victims, such as rodents and reptiles, on the ground.

► Eland

RANGE: AFRICA SOUTH OF THE SAHARA

HABITAT: SAVANNA

The eland is the largest of the antelopes. Big bulls can weigh up to a ton. Both male and female have long, straight horns up to 28 in (70 cm) long, with a spiral twist. They are browsing animals, feeding at dusk and dawn in open country with scattered trees. They not only eat leaves, but also dig up roots with their hooves.

▲ Fox, Red

RANGE: N. AMERICA, EURASIA, INTRODUCED AUSTRALIA

HABITAT: WOODLAND, GRASSLAND

Red foxes hunt at night alone and come together only to breed and rear young. They feed on a wide range of food. Their natural habitat is forest and grassland, but many have managed to adapt to suburban gardens and even city centers.

▼ Gerbil, Great

RANGE: S. EUROPE, ASIA, AFRICA

HABITAT: DESERT

Gerbils are good at living in dry places, getting most of their water from food and avoiding the heat by burrowing.

▼ Gerbil, Large North African

RANGE: N. AFRICA

HABITAT: DESERT

The North African gerbil lives in rough burrows dug in sand where it hides during the day, emerging at dusk to forage.

▼ Gibbon, Lar
RANGE: S. E. ASIA
HABITAT: FOREST
The Lar gibbon is one of nine species of apes called gibbon. Gibbons are great acrobats, using their long arms to swing through the forest canopy with amazing speed.

▲ Gibbon, Pileated
RANGE: THAILAND
HABITAT: FOREST
The pileated gibbon has a black cap of hair on its head. It is born white, and turns black from the head down as it grows older. It is strongly territorial and a male will scream and shout abuse at other males.

▶ Giraffe
RANGE: AFRICA SOUTH OF THE SAHARA
HABITAT: SAVANNA
The giraffe is the world's tallest animal, growing up to 20 ft (6 m). Half of its height is its incredibly long neck which enables it to reach the leaves and buds of acacia and thorn trees far above the ground. But it has to splay its long front legs in order to drink. Giraffes live in small groups of females and young led by a male.

▲ Glider, Greater
RANGE: E. AUSTRALIA
HABITAT: FOREST
The greater glider is the biggest of Australia's gliding possums, able to glide 330 ft (100 m) or more from tree to tree. Like all possums, it is a marsupial.

▲ Glider, Sugar
RANGE: N. E. AUSTRALIA, NEW GUINEA
HABITAT: FOREST
The sugar glider is a gliding possum that feeds on the sugary sap oozing from wounds on the bark of wattle and gum trees.

▲ Gopher, Plains pocket
RANGE: N. AMERICA
HABITAT: DESERT, GRASSLAND
The pocket gopher gets its name from its cheek pouches, which can be crammed full of food to take back to its burrow.

▼ Gorilla
RANGE: C. AFRICA
HABITAT: RAIN FOREST
The gorilla is the largest primate and the largest of the great apes, weighing up to 660 lb (300 kg). Gorillas live in forests in groups led by a large male, or silverback. Despite their size, they are gentle creatures, feeding on leaves and stems which they snap off with their hands.

▼ Guanaco
RANGE: S. AMERICA
HABITAT: GRASSLAND, MOUNTAINS
The guanaco is related to the camel and, like camels, it kneels when lying down. It is a very hardy creature, able to survive in the scorching Atacama Desert and on snowy mountains.

▼ Guinea pig
RANGE: S. AMERICA
HABITAT: GRASSLAND, ROCKS
Guinea pigs, or cavies, are small rodents that feed on grass and leaves. Cavies are the ancestors of pet guinea pigs.

▼ Hamster, Common
RANGE: EURASIA
HABITAT: GRASSLAND, FARMLAND
Hamsters are small burrowing rodents with large cheek pouches which they use for carrying food back to their burrows.

▼ Hare, Brown
RANGE: EURASIA, INTRODUCED AMERICAS, AUSTRALIA
HABITAT: WOODLAND, FARMLAND
Unlike rabbits, hares live above ground in a shallow depression called a form. They rely on speed to escape and can run at up to 30 mph (50 km/h). Their young, called leverets, can run soon after they are born.

▼ Hedgehog, Western
RANGE: W. EUROPE, INTRODUCED NEW ZEALAND
HABITAT: WOODLAND, FARMLAND
The hedgehog hibernates for up to six months a year. If threatened, it rolls up into a little ball and makes its 6,000 spines stand on end.

▼ Hippopotamus
RANGE: AFRICA SOUTH OF THE SAHARA
HABITAT: RIVERS OR LAKES IN GRASSLAND
The hippo is a huge creature, weighing up to 3 tons, with huge jaws. It lounges in water by day and emerges at night to feed on grass and other plants.

▼ Hippopotamus, Pygmy
RANGE: W. AFRICA
HABITAT: RAIN FOREST
The pygmy hippo is a small hippo with a narrower mouth and thinner body. It lives mainly on land and feeds on leaves and fallen fruit, which it forages for at night.

▲ Marten, American
RANGE: CANADA, ALASKA, N. W. U.S.A.
HABITAT: TAIGA/PINE FOREST
Martens are small, tough carnivores that live in pine forests. They are skillful climbers and adept at catching red squirrels, which they chase through the treetops. They live in dens in hollow trees or logs.

▼ Meerkat
RANGE: SOUTHERN AFRICA
HABITAT: SAVANNA
The meerkat is a small mammal that lives in burrows, linked to form a colony. It feeds on insects, spiders, scorpions, and small mammals. When aboveground, some of the group always act as lookouts, sitting upright. When cool, the meerkat sits up sunning itself; when hot, it lies belly-down in its burrow.

▲ Mink, American
RANGE: N. AMERICA, INTRODUCED BRITAIN
HABITAT: WETLAND, RIVERBANKS
There are two species of mink: the North American mink and the slightly smaller European mink. Minks are usually seen near rivers or lakes, preying on waterfowl and fish, usually at night. Because of their soft, rich brown fur they have often been trapped and farmed to make fur coats. British minks have escaped from farms.

▼ Mole, Eastern
RANGE: EASTERN N. AMERICA
HABITAT: FIELDS, LAWNS, AND GARDENS
The Eastern mole spends nearly all its life underground, digging through the soil with its powerful front paws. It is almost blind but finds the earthworms and insect grubs it feeds on with its sensitive nose.

▼ Mole, European
RANGE: EUROPE, EASTERN ASIA
HABITAT: WOODLAND, FARMLAND
The mole spends most of its life burrowing tunnels underground, so is not often seen. The only signs of its activity are the soil heaps, called mole hills, it makes while tunneling.

▼ Mole, Giant golden
RANGE: SOUTH AFRICA
HABITAT: WOODLAND
The rare giant golden mole is the biggest of all moles, up to 9½ in (24 cm) long. Unlike other moles, this mole hunts aboveground for beetles, slugs, and worms—even though it is blind, and so has to rely on smell and sound alone. When frightened, it scurries for its burrow and seems to be able to find the entrance even though it cannot see.

▼ Mole, Star-nosed
RANGE: NORTHEASTERN N. AMERICA
HABITAT: WETLAND, WOODLAND
The star-nosed mole lives in wet places. Although it digs tunnels, it rarely feeds there. It has a ring of 22 fingerlike tentacles on the end of its nose, which it uses to feel for food, such as small fish, when it is underwater.

▲ Mole-rat, Naked
RANGE: N. E. AFRICA
HABITAT: DRY SAVANNA
Naked mole-rats have pink, almost furless bodies and live underground in colonies of up to 100, controlled by a single female or queen. The queen and her fat helpers are fed by "workers."

▲ Mongoose, Indian
RANGE: SOUTHERN ASIA, INTRODUCED ELSEWHERE
HABITAT: FOREST TO DESERT
The mongoose is a swift, effective predator. It catches rats, mice, and scorpions, but it is famed for the way it attacks snakes, such as cobras.

▲ Monkey, Western red colobus
RANGE: W. AFRICA
HABITAT: RAIN FOREST
Red colobuses are five species of colobus monkeys, which are very agile African monkeys that spend almost all their lives in trees. Although they have no thumbs, they are brilliant climbers and cling on with their fingers as they dart through the treetops searching for fruit, leaves, and flowers.

▲ Monkey, Diana
RANGE: W. AFRICA
HABITAT: RAIN FOREST
The Diana monkey is a noisy little monkey that lives in troops of 30 or so in the rain forest canopy. It feeds mainly on leaves, fruit, and buds soon after dawn and just before dusk. It also eats insects and birds' eggs.

▲ Monkey, Proboscis
RANGE: S. E. ASIA, BORNEO
HABITAT: RAIN FOREST, MANGROVE SWAMPS
The male proboscis monkey gives the species its name, with its very long, pink nose. This normally dangles straight down but straightens out when he honks loudly.

▶ Monkey, Red howler
RANGE: TROPICAL S. AMERICA
HABITAT: RAIN FOREST
The howler monkey gets its name from its incredible dawn and dusk shrieks, which can be heard echoing through the trees up to 2 miles (3 km) away. Red howlers are the biggest American monkeys.

▲ Monkey, Vervet
RANGE: S. AND E. AFRICA
HABITAT: SAVANNA, WOODS
Otherwise known as the green guenon, this monkey climbs, jumps, swims well, and sleeps in trees; but it is quite happy running and foraging in open country.

▶ Monkey, Woolly spider
RANGE: S. E. BRAZIL
HABITAT: COASTAL FOREST
The woolly spider monkey has long limbs and a prehensile tail, which it uses as an extra limb to help it move through the trees. It has a bare face that becomes red when it is excited.

▲ Moose

RANGE: EURASIA, N. AMERICA
HABITAT: TAIGA, TUNDRA

The moose or elk is the biggest of all deer and the antlers of bulls may be 6 ft (1.8 m) across. Moose shed the antlers in winter and grow bigger ones in spring. Bulls bellow to attract females and engage in fierce battles with rivals.

▲ Mouflon

RANGE: S. EUROPE, C. AND S. ASIA
HABITAT: MOUNTAINS

The mouflon is a tough mountain sheep, which may be an ancestor of the domestic sheep. It seems able to eat virtually any vegetation, including plants other animals find poisonous.

▶ Mouse, Deer

RANGE: N. AMERICA
HABITAT: WOODLAND, GRASSLAND

The deer mouse makes nests underground, or in trees, where it starts to breed when only seven weeks old. It is a very nimble creature and feeds on insects, seeds, and nuts.

▼ Mouse, Wood

RANGE: EASTERN EURASIA
HABITAT: WOODLAND, FARMLAND

Also known as the long-tailed field mouse, the wood mouse may be the most common European mammal, thriving everywhere from moorlands to suburban gardens. It often nests in burrows under trees and emerges at night to scurry around, foraging for seeds. It hibernates in winter.

▲ Muntjac, Chinese

RANGE: CHINA, INTRODUCED EUROPE
HABITAT: FOREST

The muntjac is the size of a big dog and is now the smallest European deer. It is known as the "barking deer" in Asia because of its barklike cry.

▲ Musk ox

RANGE: N. CANADA, GREENLAND
HABITAT: TUNDRA

The musk ox looks like a buffalo, but is actually related to the mountain goat. It lives in the Arctic tundra and has a long, shaggy coat to help it survive the bitter winter. Its big hooves stop it from sinking in soft snow.

▲ Muskrat, Common

RANGE: N. AMERICA, INTRODUCED EUROPE
HABITAT: MARSHES, RIVERBANKS

The muskrat lives in water and eats marsh vegetation voraciously. In winter it lives in a lodge like a beaver's, only built with reeds.

◀ Myotis, Little brown

RANGE: N. AMERICA
HABITAT: FOREST, SUBURBS

This common little bat often forms nursery colonies in attics and walls of buildings. Each bat can eat more than 1,200 insects an hour.

▼ Narwhal

RANGE: HIGH ARCTIC
HABITAT: COLD OCEANS

The narwhal is a whale. The male has an extraordinary tusk, up to 10 ft (3 m) long, which is actually an extended tooth and is used to fight rival males.

▲ Numbat

RANGE: S. W. AUSTRALIA
HABITAT: FOREST

The numbat is a small marsupial, but has no pouch. The young are dragged around clinging to the mother's nipples. It feeds on termites, and licks them up with its 4 in- (10 cm-) long tongue.

▲ Okapi

RANGE: W. AFRICA
HABITAT: RAIN FOREST

The okapi looks like a horse with a zebra's stripes on its back legs. In fact, it is a relative of the giraffe and browses on leaves, twisting them off with its long tongue.

▲ Opossum, Virginia

RANGE: N. AND C. AMERICA
HABITAT: WOODLAND, FARMLAND

The Virginia opossum is one of the few marsupials outside Australia and has a kangaroo-like pouch. Scared opossums play dead.

▶ Orangutan

RANGE: SUMATRA, BORNEO
HABITAT: RAIN FOREST

The orangutan is the second largest great ape after the gorilla. Unlike gorillas, it spends most of its life in trees and builds a platform of sticks for a nest. As its rain forest habitat has shrunk, so the orangutan's survival has been threatened.

▼ Oryx, Arabian

RANGE: ARABIA
HABITAT: DESERT

The very rare Arabian oryx is well adapted to life in the desert and can endure long periods without water, getting most of its water from the plants on which it feeds. The oryx breathes deeply in the cool, moist night air to help its body make water.

▶ Otter, Eurasian

RANGE: EURASIA, N. AFRICA
HABITAT: RIVERS, LAKES, COASTS

With its streamlined body, the otter is a strong, fast swimmer, using its tail to propel it through the water. It typically lives in a burrow in the riverbank and comes out at night to hunt for fish, frogs, and voles.

▼ Otter, Sea

RANGE: N. E. PACIFIC OCEAN

HABITAT: ROCKY COASTS

The sea otter spends most of its life at sea. It stays in shallow water close to beds of giant kelp seaweed. To eat shellfish, it floats on its back, rests a stone on its belly, and smashes the shellfish against the stone until the shell breaks.

▼ Panda, Giant

RANGE: C. CHINA

HABITAT: FOREST

The rare giant panda has the digestive system of a meat-eater, but actually feeds only on the shoots of bamboo plants, which it eats sitting down, gripping the bamboo in its front paws.

▼ Panda, Red

RANGE: S. ASIA, CHINA

HABITAT: MOUNTAIN FOREST

The red panda looks a little like a raccoon. It sleeps during the day curled up on branches with its tail wrapped around to keep it warm. It comes down to the ground at night to feed on bamboo shoots, grass, roots, fruit, acorns, and occasionally mice. When angry it rears up and hisses.

▲ Pangolin, Giant

RANGE: E. AND C. AFRICA

HABITAT: RAIN FOREST, SAVANNA

Pangolins are the only mammals covered in scales. When threatened they roll themselves up into a ball and raise their scales so the sharp edges point outward. They feed on ants and termites, which they lick up with their long, sticky tongues. They have thick eyelids to protect their eyes from ant bites and can seal off their nostrils to keep the ants out.

◄ Pangolin, Tree

RANGE: W. AFRICA

HABITAT: RAIN FOREST

Like all pangolins, the tree pangolin is covered in scales, but it is also a good climber with a long, prehensile tail. It often sleeps on the ground during the day and climbs up trees to hunt ants by smell at night.

▼ Peccary, Collared

RANGE: N., C., AND S. AMERICA

HABITAT: FOREST, GRASSLAND, DESERT

Peccaries are piglike mammals that forage for a wide range of food, from insects to prickly pear cacti. The collared peccary is the most widespread of all peccaries.

▼ Pika, Northern

RANGE: N. ASIA

HABITAT: MOUNTAINS, FOREST

The pika is like a rabbit without the big ears, but it usually lives high up in mountains. In summer it builds up little haystacks of grass among the rocks to eat during winter.

▲ Platypus

RANGE: E. AUSTRALIA, TASMANIA

HABITAT: LAKES AND RIVERS

The platypus is one of the few mammals that lays eggs. It also has webbed feet and a bill like a duck, which it uses to probe riverbed mud for insect grubs.

▲ Polecat, Western

RANGE: EUROPE

HABITAT: FOREST

The Western polecat is a small carnivore related to stoats and weasels. It hunts rodents, birds, and lizards at night.

► Porcupine, Crested

RANGE: AFRICA SOUTH OF THE SAHARA

HABITAT: FOREST, SAVANNA

This is a big rodent, armed with fearsome spines, called quills, on its back, measuring up to 12 in (30.5 cm) long. If threatened, it rattles its tail quills and charges backward, spines raised, at its foe.

▼ Possum, Brush-tailed

RANGE: AUSTRALIA, INTRODUCED NEW ZEALAND

HABITAT: WOODLAND

This is a nimble, tree-climbing marsupial that feeds mainly on leaves, flowers, and fruit. It is now quite at home in urban areas.

▲ Potoroo

RANGE: AUSTRALIA

HABITAT: DAMP SCRUB, GRASSLAND

Potoroos are small, ratlike kangaroos with soft, silky fur. Like larger kangaroos, they bound along on their strong back legs. They eat a much wider range of food than larger kangaroos, including plants, plant roots, grass, fungi, and insects, which they forage for at dusk.

▼ Prairie dog, Black-tailed

RANGE: C. U.S.A.

HABITAT: PRAIRIE

This squirrel lives in huge networks of burrows called townships. It gets its name from its doglike bark.

▼ Pronghorn

RANGE: W. U.S.A.

HABITAT: PRAIRIE

The world's fastest hoofed mammal, this can reach over 60 mph (100 km/h). Its eyes are so good it can spot movements 4 miles (6.5 km) away.

▲ Quokka

RANGE: S. W. AUSTRALIA

HABITAT: DENSE VEGETATION

Once widespread, quokkas were shot for sport and now live in few places other than Rottnest Island. This island got its name, which means "Rat's Nest," because European explorers thought the quokkas were rats.

▲ Quoll, Eastern

RANGE: S. E. AUSTRALIA, TASMANIA

HABITAT: FOREST

Quolls are a family of lithe, catlike marsupials that live in forests in Australia and New Guinea. They live in trees and hunt lizards and birds.

▲ Rabbit, European

RANGE: EUROPE, INTRODUCED ELSEWHERE

HABITAT: GRASSLAND, WOODLAND, FARMLAND

Rabbits live in burrows and breed very fast, with several litters a year. They eat grass and can also wreak havoc with farmers' crops of vegetables and grains.

▲ Raccoon

RANGE: N. AND C. AMERICA

HABITAT: WOODLAND, SUBURBS

The raccoon is a woodland creature, but has learned to scavenge from humans and is renowned for its night raids on garbage cans. Its name is Native American for "scratches with hands."

▲ Rat, Arizona cotton

RANGE: SOUTHEASTERN U.S.A.

HABITAT: DRY GRASSLAND

Cotton rat populations sometimes expand so much that they are declared a plague. They normally feed on plants and small insects but may also feed on quail eggs.

▲ Rat, Baja California rice

RANGE: MEXICO, CALIFORNIA

HABITAT: MARSHLAND

Rice rats generally live in marshland and feed on reeds and sedges, and sometimes on fish. They sometimes also eat rice crops and can become serious pests.

▲ Rat, Brown

RANGE: WORLDWIDE

HABITAT: CITIES, HOUSES, FARMLAND

Also known as the Norway rat, the brown rat originally came from S. E. Asia, but has spread with human habitation around the world. It eats almost anything.

▲ Rat, Swamp

RANGE: S. AFRICA

HABITAT: SWAMPS

The swamp rat feeds on seeds, berries, and fruits and lives in nests made of reeds and grasses.

▼ Rhebok

RANGE: S. AFRICA

HABITAT: GRASSLAND

The rhebok is a small antelope with soft hair. The ram (male) is aggressively territorial, marking out his range by clicking his tongue, whistling, and urinating.

▲ Rhinoceros, Black

RANGE: AFRICA SOUTH OF THE SAHARA

HABITAT: SAVANNA

Unlike their Asian cousins, Africa's black and white rhinos have two horns. The black is slightly smaller than the white and has a pointed upper lip to eat leaves—unlike the white, which has a wide lip for grazing.

▲ Sable

RANGE: N. ASIA

HABITAT: TAIGA

This small weasel-like predator eats small mammals, fish, nuts, and berries. Its thick, soft fur insulates it against the icy Siberian winters, but has meant it is widely trapped for its fur.

▲ Saiga

RANGE: C. ASIA

HABITAT: STEPPE

The saiga is a goat-antelope with a trunklike nose that may filter out dust from the air in the summer and warm frosty air in the bitter steppe winter.

▼ Saki, Monk

RANGE: AMAZON

HABITAT: RAIN FOREST

Saki monkeys are a family of long-tailed S. American monkeys with long, coarse hair. The monk saki has long, shaggy hair around its face and neck which looks like a monk's cowl. It is a wary monkey that lives high in the forest canopy and rarely ventures down to the ground, clambering along branches on all fours. Occasionally it walks upright on large boughs and makes huge leaps from branch to branch.

▼ Sea lion, California

RANGE: W. U.S.A.

HABITAT: COASTS

The California sea lion is the trained seal—playful and brilliant at balancing and catching things in the air with its teeth. It is also very fast, able to swim at speeds of 25 mph (40 km/h), and can dive down 500 ft (150 m) for fish. Like all sea lions, it has front flippers strong enough to support its weight, and it can move quickly on land, almost galloping— unlike seals that only shuffle. It barks, wails, and bleats.

▲ Snake, Western blind
RANGE: S. W. U.S.A.
HABITAT: DESERT
This snake looks a little like an earthworm. It has black spots where its eyes should be, but it is actually totally blind. It tracks ants and termites by following their scent trails.

▲ Soft-shell, Spiny
RANGE: N. AMERICA
HABITAT: RIVERS, CREEKS, PONDS
Unlike other turtles, soft-shells have shells of skin rather than horny plates. Spiny soft-shells are great swimmers that can make a fast getaway if threatened when basking on a sand bar.

▲ Terrapin, River
RANGE: S. E. ASIA
HABITAT: TIDAL RIVERS
Also known as the batagur, this is a plant-eating turtle that nests on sand banks where it lays 50 eggs at a time. People have dug up so many of its eggs for food that it is now quite rare.

▼ Tortoise, African pancake
RANGE: E. AFRICA
HABITAT: ROCKY OUTCROPS
This tortoise gets its name from its shell, which is soft and flat. It does not retreat into its shell when threatened, but wedges itself into a rock crevice by inflating its lungs.

▼ Tortoise, Spur-thighed
RANGE: N. AFRICA, S. EUROPE, S. W. ASIA
HABITAT: MEADOWS
The spur-thighed tortoise has large spurs on its thighs, but otherwise is very similar to the highly domed Hermann's tortoise of southeastern Europe, for which it is often mistaken.

▼ Tortoise, Galapagos giant
RANGE: GALAPAGOS ISLANDS
HABITAT: VARIED
The Galapagos giant tortoise is the biggest of all tortoises, weighing up to 770 lbs (350 kg). It lives on land and feeds on almost any plant, especially cacti. It can live for over 100 years, but in the past many were killed by sailors for food. At least 13 subspecies of giant tortoise have evolved on the islands of the Galapagos group. The subspecies vary in size, length, and shape of the carapace (shell).

▲ Tuatara, Cook-Strait
RANGE: NEW ZEALAND
HABITAT: WOODS
The two species of tuatara are unique reptiles found only in New Zealand— the last survivors of an ancient group called rhynchocephalians (beak heads). Unusually, tuataras do not breed until they are at least 20 years old.

▲ Turtle, Alligator snapping
RANGE: MISSISSIPPI VALLEY, U.S.A.
HABITAT: DEEP RIVERS, LAKES
This is the largest freshwater turtle. It lurks on riverbeds with its mouth gaping to reveal a wiggling, pink appendage, which fish come to investigate. They are then snapped up by the turtle.

▲ Turtle, Green
RANGE: WORLDWIDE
HABITAT: WARM SEAS ABOVE 68°F (20°C)
This is one of the few turtles that spends nearly all its life at sea. At nesting time it swims thousands of miles to lay its eggs on the beach where it was born. It lays its eggs on sandy beaches, hauling itself ashore at night.

▲ Turtle, Loggerhead
RANGE: PACIFIC, INDIAN, ATLANTIC OCEANS
HABITAT: COASTAL WATERS
In the summer breeding season the female loggerhead comes ashore at night and digs her nest at the foot of sand dunes, laying up to five clutches, each of about 100 eggs. Sadly numbers of loggerheads have been reduced by coastal development and fishing nets.

▼ Turtle, Murray River
RANGE: S. E. AUSTRALIA
HABITAT: RIVERS
Unusually, the shape of this turtle's carapace (shell) changes as it grows. When it hatches, the shell is round, then it grows at the back, and finally becomes oval in adult turtles.

▼ Turtle, Wood
RANGE: N. E. U.S.A., GREAT LAKES
HABITAT: WOODS, MEADOWS, MARSHES
The wood turtle spends most of its life on land and is a good climber, feeding on fruit, worms, slugs, and insects. It is a popular pet but has been hunted so much that it is now rare in the wild.

▼ Viper, Common
RANGE: EURASIA
HABITAT: MOORS, HEATHS, SCRUB
Known in Britain as adders, vipers are venomous snakes, but they are very timid and rarely bite humans. They hibernate in winter but emerge only when it gets warmer than 46°F (8°C).

▼ Viper, Gaboon
RANGE: W. C. AND S. E. AFRICA
HABITAT: RAIN FOREST, WOODLAND
The two species of gaboon viper are among the largest vipers, growing up to 6 ft (1.8 m) long. They are slow-moving and often lie in wait for their prey, which include rats, squirrels, and even small antelopes.

Amphibians

Like reptiles, amphibians are cold-blooded, but have no scales, and their skin is kept moist by secretions from mucus glands. Most amphibians begin life in water, or in a fluid-filled egg sac, and have gills to help them breathe in water. As they develop, they leave the water and spend their adult lives on land. Most of the 4,780 species live in the tropics, and there are three main kinds: frogs and toads (over 4,000 species), salamanders (410), and caecilians (165).

▼ Axolotl
RANGE: LAKE XOCHIMILCO, MEXICO
HABITAT: MOUNTAIN LAKES
Axolotl is Aztec for "water monster." Uniquely, this salamander never grows up fully. Although it grows four legs, it remains a tadpole all its life, even breeding in this state.

▼ Bullfrog
RANGE: N. AMERICA, MEXICO
HABITAT: LAKES, PONDS, SLOW STREAMS
As big as a young rabbit, the bullfrog is an awesome predator, snapping up other frogs, small snakes, fish, and even songbirds. Its call is a grumbling, throaty croak.

▼ Caecilian, South American
RANGE: S. AMERICA
HABITAT: USUALLY FOREST
Caecilians look like earthworms, but they are actually amphibians. Most live in soft soil in rain forests and tunnel through the soil feeding on worms, insects, and centipedes.

▲ Eel, Congo two-toed
RANGE: S. E. U.S.A.
HABITAT: SWAMPS, BAYOUS
Congo eels look like eels but are salamanders and live in the southeast U.S., not the Congo. The two-toed Congo eel has tiny, useless legs with two toes.

▲ Ensatina
RANGE: WESTERN N. AMERICA
HABITAT: FORESTS, UNDER LOGS AND ROCKS
Ensatinas are a varied group of small salamanders. One feature they all share is a narrow base to their tails. If the tail snaps off when escaping a predator, it grows back after two years.

▲ Frog, Common
RANGE: N. EUROPE, W. ASIA
HABITAT: MOIST AREAS NEAR PONDS
The common frog lives mostly on land, but in spring returns to ponds to mate. Each female lays 3–4,000 jelly-coated eggs that float in the ponds in large masses called frogspawn.

▼ Frog, Corroboree
RANGE: NEW SOUTH WALES (AUSTRALIA)
HABITAT: MOUNTAINS, MARSHES
With its striking yellow and black markings, the corroboree frog is instantly recognizable, but there are now fewer than 300 of them left in their habitat in the Snowy Mountains.

▼ Frog, Darwin's
RANGE: SOUTHERN S. AMERICA
HABITAT: COLD STREAMS IN FORESTS
Unusually, the eggs of the Darwin's frog are cared for by the male. After the female lays the eggs, the male gulps in a dozen or so and keeps them safe in the croaking sac in his throat until they hatch.

▼ Frog, European green tree
RANGE: EUROPE, W. ASIA
HABITAT: TREES, BUSHES NEAR LAKES
The European green tree frog is one of the few tree frogs that live outside the tropics. It is a great climber with sticky pads on its toes for clinging on to trees. It feeds mainly on insects.

▲ Frog, Glass
RANGE: NORTHERN S. AMERICA
HABITAT: RAIN FOREST
Glass frogs get their name because most have semitransparent skin on the underside, so making their internal organs clearly visible. They spend their lives in trees and are great climbers. They lay their eggs on leaves above pools and streams, so that the tadpoles can drop into the water as they hatch and burrow into the mud on the stream bed.

▲ Frog, Golden poison arrow
RANGE: C. AND S. AMERICA
HABITAT: RAIN FOREST
There are about 100 species of poison arrow frogs, most of which are brilliantly colored like the golden poison arrow frog. Glands on their skin contain deadly poisons used by forest peoples to tip their arrows for hunting. The brilliant colors warn predators that they are poisonous, so that they can feed in broad daylight.

▲ Frog, Horned
RANGE: NORTHERN S. AMERICA
HABITAT: RAIN FOREST
The Amazonian horned frog has a plump body that is as wide as it is long. It cannot move very fast, so hides in leaf litter on the forest floor until its prey passes by. Its mouth is so large that it can catch animals that are almost as big as itself, such as small frogs and rodents. The "horns" are projections on its eyelids.

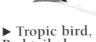

▶ Tropic bird, Red-tailed

RANGE: INDIAN AND PACIFIC OCEANS

HABITAT: OCEANS

With its long, dark red tail feathers, the red-tailed tropic bird is an unusual-looking seabird. In the breeding season it goes slightly pink.

▲ Turaco, Red-crested

RANGE: AFRICA

HABITAT: FOREST, SAVANNA

Turacos are colorful African relatives of cuckoos. They live in tropical forests and feed on fruit. The red-crested turaco is a poor flier, but runs, hops, and climbs very nimbly and swiftly through the branches of rain forest trees.

▲ Turkey, Wild

RANGE: U.S.A., MEXICO

HABITAT: WOODED COUNTRY, SCRUB

Wild turkeys are big fowl that strut around woodlands in groups of 20 or so for most of the year, foraging for seeds, nuts, and berries. They are strong fliers over short distances and roost in trees.

▲ Vireo, Red-eyed

RANGE: BREEDS N. AMERICA; WINTERS S. AMERICA

HABITAT: FOREST

The red-eyed vireo is a tireless songster, singing right through the day. It builds a neat cup-shaped nest in a tree fork. Nestlings leave the nest after 12 days.

▼ Vulture, King

RANGE: C. AND S. AMERICA

HABITAT: RAIN FOREST, SAVANNA

Like the giant condors of California and the Andes, the king vulture is one of seven American vulture species. Like African vultures it feeds on carrion and has a bald head for plunging into messy carcasses. But unlike African vultures, king and other American vultures are related to storks, not birds of prey. The king vulture relies on smell to track prey.

▼ Vulture, Lappet-faced

RANGE: AFRICA, MIDDLE EAST

HABITAT: SAVANNA, DESERT

This is the biggest of the African vultures and, though often last to arrive at a carcass, it pushes the other vultures out of the way. With its big, powerful beak it can cut easily through flesh and its bald head saves its plumage from getting soiled with blood.

▲ Warbler, Willow

RANGE: BREEDS EURASIA; WINTERS AFRICA, S. ASIA

HABITAT: WOODLAND, FARMLAND

The willow warbler is one of more than 300 warblers spread widely across Eurasia and Australia. All mainly eat insects and each has a distinctive song.

▲ Warbler, Yellow

RANGE: BREEDS N. AMERICA; WINTERS C. AND S. AMERICA

HABITAT: THICKETS BY STREAMS, SWAMPS

The yellow warbler is one of the most widespread of American wood warblers. Like all warblers it forages in trees for insects.

▲ Wigeon, American

RANGE: BREEDS NORTHERN N. AMERICA; WINTERS IN THE SOUTH

HABITAT: MARSHES

Wigeons are called dabbling ducks, but they find very little food by dabbling. Usually they graze on grass in marshes in huge, tightly packed flocks. They may even snatch the food of other diving birds.

▲ Woodcock, American

RANGE: BREEDS N. AMERICA; WINTERS TO THE SOUTH

HABITAT: WOODLAND

Woodcocks are actually waders but they have left the shore to live in woods where they probe soft soil for worms with their long bills.

▼ Woodcreeper, Long-billed

RANGE: S. AMERICA

HABITAT: RAIN FOREST

This bird is one of 49 species of woodcreepers in the Americas. They are the equivalent of the treecreepers of Africa and, like them, climb trees, picking insects from crevices in the bark.

▶ Woodpecker, Pileated

RANGE: N. AMERICA

HABITAT: FOREST

Woodpeckers feed mainly on ants and termites and find their food by clinging to tree trunks with their sharp claws and hammering away with their strong beaks. The pileated woodpecker can often be heard drumming on trees in woods.

▼ Wren

RANGE: EURASIA, N. AFRICA

HABITAT: WOODLAND, FARMLAND

Wrens are tiny songbirds with short, upright tails that hop about the ground searching for insects and spiders. They nest in hollow tree stumps or among tree roots.

▼ Zitting cisticola

RANGE: SOUTHERN EURASIA, N. AFRICA, AUSTRALIA

HABITAT: DAMP GRASSLAND, RICE FIELDS

This little warbler is well known for the male's song flight, during which it spirals up to 100 ft (30 m) above the ground while singing.

Invertebrates

Creatures without backbones, such as insects, snails, and worms are called invertebrates. Most invertebrates are small, but there are more of them than all other animals put together. Of the world's million and a half known animal species, a million are insects, and there are huge numbers of other invertebrates living on land—including centipedes, arachnids such as spiders, and crustaceans such as woodlice.

▶ Bee, Cuckoo

RANGE: WORLDWIDE

HABITAT: NEAR FLOWERS

Cuckoo bees cannot carry pollen so, like cuckoo birds, they lay their eggs in the nests of others—in this case, bees. The cuckoo bees' eggs hatch first and the larvae eat up their host's food store.

▲ Ant, Army

RANGE: C. AND S. AMERICA

HABITAT: RAIN FOREST

Unlike other ants, army ants do not make a permanent nest. Instead they crawl across the forest floor, devouring any small creature in their path and then spend the night in a temporary nest called a bivouac, with walls made by ants clinging to each other.

▲ Ant, Carpenter

RANGE: WORLDWIDE

HABITAT: WOOD

Colonies of carpenter ants make their nests in wooden buildings or in rotting tree trunks. The nests can destroy the timber in roofs or walls.

▶ Ant, Fire

RANGE: S. AMERICA, INTRODUCED N. AMERICA

HABITAT: WOODS, FIELDS

Fire ants get their name because they inflict a very painful bite, which they use to attack other insects. They were introduced into Alabama from South America and are now major pests because they build huge nests, damage grain, and attack poultry.

▼ Ant, Harvester

RANGE: WORLDWIDE

HABITAT: FIELDS

These ants get their name from their habit of gathering seeds and storing them in special granary areas in the nest, ready to eat in times of need.

▼ Ant, Leafcutter

RANGE: C. AND S. AMERICA

HABITAT: RAIN FOREST

Leafcutter ants spend the night in nests under the rain forest floor, then at dawn workers crawl out and climb trees to cut pieces of leaves to bring back to the nest. Instead of eating the leaves, they use them to make a compost on which a fungus grows. They eat the fungus.

▼ Ant, Red wood

RANGE: EURASIA

HABITAT: WOODLAND

By preying on plant-eating insects, wood ants play a key role in reducing the damage done to forest trees. Wood ants also feed on the sticky honeydew secreted by aphids.

▼ Ant, Velvet

RANGE: WORLDWIDE, ESPECIALLY TROPICS

HABITAT: VARIED

These are not ants but wasps, covered with velvety hair. They get their name because the females are wingless and antlike.

▲ Ant lion

RANGE: WORLDWIDE, ESPECIALLY TROPICS

HABITAT: SCRUB AND DRY, SANDY AREAS

Ant lions get their name from their larvae, which dig a pit in sandy soil to trap ants. When an ant comes near, the larvae tosses soil at it so that it falls into the trap.

▼ Aphid

RANGE: WORLDWIDE

HABITAT: GREEN PLANTS

Aphids are tiny insects that feed on the sap of leaves and plants and can do great damage. They multiply rapidly, but may be eaten by ladybugs and wasps.

▼ Bedbug

RANGE: WORLDWIDE

HABITAT: HUMAN AND ANIMAL HOSTS, CREVICES

Bedbugs stay hidden during the day, but come out at night to feed on the blood of birds and animals, including humans.

▶ Bee, Carpenter

RANGE: WORLDWIDE

HABITAT: NEAR FLOWERS

Female carpenter bees chew into wood, making a tunnel-like nest for their brood cell. They line the nest with sticky pollen, lay a single egg, then seal the cell.

▲ Bee, Leafcutter

RANGE: WORLDWIDE

HABITAT: VARIED

Leafcutter bees live alone rather than in swarms. They cut out pieces of leaf with their jaws and use them to line their nests—usually a tunnel in rotting wood.

▲ Bee, Mining

RANGE: WORLDWIDE EXCEPT AUSTRALIA

HABITAT: NEAR SPRING FLOWERS

The mines of mining bees are long, branching tunnels they dig into the ground. They stock them with nectar and pollen for their larvae to eat when they hatch.

▲ Cockroach, German

RANGE: WORLDWIDE

HABITAT: LEAF LITTER, GARBAGE, BUILDINGS
The German cockroach is a common pest in kitchens and food stores. It multiplies rapidly. Unlike common cockroaches, such as the American, it has proper wings.

► Cockroach, Madagascan hissing

RANGE: MADAGASCAR

HABITAT: RAIN FOREST
Males of this species fight each other. When they win they often hiss by squeezing air out of the breathing holes on their bodies called spiracles. Males also hiss to court females.

▲ Crane fly

RANGE: WORLDWIDE

HABITAT: TYPICALLY NEAR WATER
Crane flies look like large, long-legged mosquitoes, but they do not bite. In fact, they do not eat anything at all because they do all their eating when they are larvae.

▲ Cricket, Mole

RANGE: WORLDWIDE

HABITAT: DAMP SAND OR SOIL NEAR STREAMS
Looking remarkably like tiny moles, mole crickets are covered in velvety hairs and burrow through the ground with their large, spadelike legs.

▼ Cricket, True

RANGE: WORLDWIDE

HABITAT: WOODLAND, ON THE GROUND IN MEADOWS
True crickets "sing" to attract mates by rubbing together special ridges at the base of their forewings. The sound is a high-pitched chirrup.

▼ Damselfly

RANGE: WORLDWIDE

HABITAT: SWAMPS, BOGS, POOLS
Damselflies, such as stalk- or spread-winged damselflies, are related to dragonflies but they are smaller and thinner. When they rest, they cling vertically to stalks with their wings out.

◄ Damselfly, Narrow-winged

RANGE: N. HEMISPHERE

HABITAT: PONDS, BOGS, STREAMS
Damselflies feed on small insects on plants. The narrow-winged damselfly folds its wings together when at rest on stalks.

▼ Darter

RANGE: WORLDWIDE

HABITAT: VARIED, INCLUDING MOUNTAIN FOREST NEAR STREAMS
Darter, or skimmer, dragonflies get their name from their fast, darting flight, often skimming just over the surface of the water as they pursue their prey.

► Dragonfly, Club-tailed

RANGE: WORLDWIDE

HABITAT: PONDS, LAKES, RIVERS
Unlike other dragonflies, the club-tailed dragonfly spots its prey by watching from a perch. Once it sights its prey, it darts out to seize it, then returns to the perch.

▼ Dragonfly, Darner

RANGE: WORLDWIDE

HABITAT: SLUGGISH WATER
Darners, also known as hawkers, include some of the largest, most powerful, and fast flying of all dragonflies. When hunting, they zoom back and forth prepared to seize their prey.

▼ Dysedera crocata

RANGE: WORLDWIDE

HABITAT: CREVICES IN WOOD
Most spiders have eight eyes; dysderid spiders like crocata have only six, set in a circle. The crocata spends the day hiding under stones, then comes out at night to hunt woodlice. This spider can pierce a woodlouse's tough body armor with its huge fangs.

▼ Earthworm

RANGE: WORLDWIDE

HABITAT: MOSTLY DAMP SOIL
Earthworms are the most common of the segmented worm group. As they tunnel into the ground, they swallow soil and digest dead leaves and rotting plant matter, then excrete the rest. This mixes up the soil and helps to keep it fertile.

▲ Earwig, Common

RANGE: ORIGINALLY EUROPE, NOW WORLDWIDE

HABITAT: VARIED
Earwigs eat plants and other insects. They have pincers at the end of their body to catch prey. They often live in flowers and are considered garden pests.

▲ Earwig, Long-horned

RANGE: WORLDWIDE, MAINLY TROPICS

HABITAT: SHORES, LEAF LITTER, DEBRIS
Also known as striped earwigs, long-horned earwigs are nocturnal, coming out at night to prey on other insects. If attacked, they squirt out a foul-smelling liquid.

▲ Firebrat

RANGE: WORLDWIDE

HABITAT: HOT, DAMP PLACES
Firebrats are a kind of silverfish. They live in hot places in buildings, such as near ovens and hot pipes. They run quickly and scurry around finding crumbs of food to eat.

▲ Firefly

RANGE: WORLDWIDE

HABITAT: WOODLAND, MOIST GRASSLAND

Fireflies, or lightning bugs, emit flashes of cold, green light when mating. The males fly, flashing, just above the ground and females flash back from the ground or trees to guide the males toward them.

▲ Flea, Cat

RANGE: WORLDWIDE

HABITAT: ON CATS

Fleas are tiny insects that live on mammals and feed on their blood. They have no wings, but they are amazing jumpers, able to jump 200 times their own length to get from host to host. Cat fleas are the most common in homes, biting people and dogs, as well as cats.

▲ Flea, Chigoe

RANGE: AMERICAS, TROPICAL

HABITAT: MAMMAL AND BIRD HOSTS

Chigoe fleas—also called jiggers—are parasites that attack various animals, including humans. Typically, pregnant females burrow into people's feet where the flea causes a reaction that makes the skin of the foot grow to engulf the insect. When the fleas hatch, they drop off their host and spend the rest of their life on the ground.

▼ Fly, Fruit

RANGE: WORLDWIDE

HABITAT: TYPICALLY FRUIT

Fruit flies feed on nectar from flowers and the juice of overripe fruit. Some species lay their eggs on the skin of fruit, such as oranges, and the larvae eat away the fruit.

▼ Fly, House

RANGE: WORLDWIDE

HABITAT: FLOWERS, DUNG, GARBAGE

House flies are among the most numerous animals on Earth. They suck liquid from anything sweet or rotting. Typically their larvae grow up in dung or garbage.

▼ Fly, Hover

RANGE: WORLDWIDE

HABITAT: TYPICALLY FLAT-TOPPED FLOWERS

Hover flies are amazing fliers, able to dart this way and that, backward and forward as they search for flowers to sip for nectar. Some hover flies deter predators by mimicking wasps.

▼ Fly, Large caddis

RANGE: MAINLY N. HEMISPHERE

HABITAT: NEAR PONDS, LAKES, RIVERS

Caddis flies look a little like moths, but their bodies are covered in hair, not scales. Females typically lay strings of eggs encased in jelly on plants just below the water surface. The larvae transform to adults and then emerge from the water.

▲ Fly, Robber

RANGE: WORLDWIDE

HABITAT: VARIED, ESPECIALLY DRY GRASSLAND

These are fast-flying, powerful insects that catch and kill other insects in midair, or pounce on them on the ground. They stab their victims through the neck and suck them dry.

▲ Froghopper

RANGE: WORLDWIDE, ESPECIALLY TROPICS

HABITAT: SHRUBS, TREES

These little insects can jump like tiny frogs. They lay their eggs on plant stems. When the nymphs hatch they cover themselves in a foam a little like saliva.

▲ Grasshopper, Long-horned

RANGE: WARM AREAS WORLDWIDE

HABITAT: TYPICALLY IN GRASS

Grasshoppers are part of a large order called Orthoptera, along with crickets, katydids, and locusts. Grasshoppers and locusts are vegetarians, feeding mainly on plants.

▼ Grasshopper, Short-horned

RANGE: WARM AREAS WORLDWIDE

HABITAT: TYPICALLY IN GRASS

Short-horned grasshoppers have short antennae. Like all grasshoppers, they have powerful back legs, which they use to jump huge distances, aided by their small wings.

▼ Harvestman

RANGE: WORLDWIDE, MAINLY TEMPERATE

HABITAT: UNDER STONES, IN LEAF LITTER

Harvestmen look like spiders, but their bodies are more oval and have no waist. They feed on small insects, such as springtails, but do not spin a web.

▼ Head louse

RANGE: WORLDWIDE

HABITAT: ON HUMANS, APES, MONKEYS

The head louse is a small, flat insect. It clings on to its host's hairs with its strongly clawed legs and then sucks on their blood.

▲ Honeybee, Western

RANGE: WORLDWIDE, EXCEPT SOUTHERN AFRICA

HABITAT: NEAR FLOWERS

Honeybees are very similar to bumblebees, but smaller and more slender. The western honeybee is the best known honeybee. Originally from Asia, it has now spread around the world—partly because it makes honey, partly because it helps to pollinate flowers.

▲ Hornet, Giant

RANGE: EURASIA, N. AMERICA

HABITAT: WOODLAND

Hornets belong to a group of insects called social wasps and live in huge paper nests made from chewed wood. In the nest, the colony is controlled by a queen. Hornets have a dangerous sting and prey on other insects; they also sip nectar.

▲ Horsefly

RANGE: WORLDWIDE

HABITAT: NEAR MAMMALS

Horseflies have huge iridescent eyes. Males feed on nectar and pollen, but the females feed on the blood of mammals—not only horses but deer, humans, and other large mammals. These flies may spread disease from animal to animal.

▼ Katydid

RANGE: WORLDWIDE, MAINLY TROPICS

HABITAT: ON VEGETATION, IN FORESTS

Also called bush crickets, katydids are narrow grasshoppers that look a little like green leaves and are hard to spot on the bushes where they live. They get their name from the song of the northern katydid male; it sounds like "Katy did."

▼ Lacewing, Green

RANGE: WORLDWIDE, ESPECIALLY DRY AREAS

HABITAT: VEGETATION, ANTS' NESTS

Lacewings prey on aphids, thrips, and mites when they fly at night. They are attracted to lights and may come into houses to hibernate in fall.

▼ Ladybug

RANGE: WORLDWIDE

HABITAT: ON LEAVES

Ladybugs are small beetles. Because they feed on aphids that destroy plants they are greatly valued as pest controllers. The ladybug's bright colors warn enemies that it tastes unpleasant.

▼ Leafhopper, Scarlet-and-green

RANGE: WORLDWIDE

HABITAT: ANYWHERE WITH VEGETATION

The scarlet-and-green leafhopper is a brilliantly colored insect. It feeds on plant juices and has powerful back legs to help it hop from plant to plant.

▼ Leaf insect

RANGE: TROPICAL ASIA, AUSTRALIA

HABITAT: LEAVES

These strange-looking insects are shaped just like the leaves they live on, right down to the veins. Even their eggs look like plant seeds, so they are hard for predators to spot.

▲ Locust, Desert

RANGE: AFRICA, ASIA

HABITAT: WARM PLACES

Locusts are plant-eating grasshoppers. The most well-known is the desert locust. In certain weather conditions, billions of insects gather together in a swarm, which can devastate crops when the locusts land and begin to feed.

▲ Louse, Bark

RANGE: WORLDWIDE

HABITAT: ON BARK

Bark lice are not part of the same insect order as body lice. In fact, most of them have wings. Most live on the bark of trees and feed on lichen and algae. Similar insects called book lice feed on paper and stored food.

▲ Louse, Feather

RANGE: WORLDWIDE

HABITAT: ON BIRDS

Feather lice are the bird equivalent of head lice. They have two claws on each leg, which they use to cling on to their host's feathers. They feed by biting off pieces of feather with their strong jaws.

▲ Mantis, Angola

RANGE: ANGOLA

HABITAT: TROPICAL RAIN FOREST

The Angola mantis is almost impossible to see on a lichen-covered branch. It waits motionless for prey, then strikes in an instant.

▲ Mantis, Flower

RANGE: TROPICS WORLDWIDE EXCEPT AUSTRALIA

HABITAT: VEGETATION

Flower mantises prey on the insects that live on flowers. They are often colored to help them hide on the flower.

▲ Mantis, Praying

RANGE: WORLDWIDE, MAINLY WARMER PLACES

HABITAT: VEGETATION

Praying mantises are deadly hunters that catch their prey by remaining perfectly still, then striking suddenly. While they wait they hold their powerful front legs together as if they are praying.

▲ Mantisfly

RANGE: WORLDWIDE, MAINLY WARM REGIONS

HABITAT: LUSH VEGETATION

Mantisflies are relatives of lacewings, but they look exactly like small praying mantises and use their front legs to seize prey in just the same way.

▲ Mayfly

RANGE: WORLDWIDE

HABITAT: STREAMS, RIVERS, PONDS

Mayflies live for several years as nymphs underwater, feeding on algae, but once they leave the water as adults they cannot eat, and they die in a few hours—just enough time to mate and lay eggs.

▲ Midge, Non-biting

RANGE: WORLDWIDE

HABITAT: NEAR PONDS, STREAMS

Midges are tiny flies that are either biting or nonbiting. Both are seen in swarms at dusk. Biting midges suck blood and have a very irritating bite.

▲ Millipede, Armored

RANGE: N. HEMISPHERE

HABITAT: LEAF LITTER

Armored, or flat-backed, millipedes have an unusually flat shape for a millipede. If attacked when crawling through the leaf litter, they can spray poisonous chemicals.

▲ Millipede, Cylinder

RANGE: MAINLY N. HEMISPHERE

HABITAT: LEAF LITTER, ROTTING WOOD

Millipedes are not insects, but long creatures in a class of their own. They move through leaf litter and eat plants.

▼ Mite, House dust

RANGE: WORLDWIDE

HABITAT: HOUSES

Mites are a huge group of tiny arachnids (like spiders). House dust mites feed on scales of skin found in house dust and their droppings can often cause allergic reactions.

▼ Mite, Velvet

RANGE: WORLDWIDE, ESPECIALLY TROPICS

HABITAT: MOSTLY IN OR ON SOIL

Velvet mites have red or orange velvety bodies. They live in the soil and feed mostly on insect eggs. At certain times of year, usually after rain, adults emerge to mate.

▼ Moth, Atlas

RANGE: SOUTHERN ASIA

HABITAT: TROPICAL FOREST

With wings measuring 12 in (30.5 cm) across, this is one of the world's largest moths. Its wings are richly colored and each has two triangular windows that are almost transparent.

▶ Moth, Bee sphinx

RANGE: AUSTRALIA

HABITAT: GRASSLAND

The bee sphinx, or hawk, moth flies by day and looks remarkably like a bee as it hovers, sipping nectar from flowers. Bee sphinx caterpillars feed on the leaves of canthium.

▲ Moth, Clothes

RANGE: WORLDWIDE

HABITAT: CLOTHES STORES, ANIMAL NESTS

Clothes moths are small moths that often spend their whole lives in houses. They lay their eggs on woolen clothes and the caterpillars live inside tents of silk, making holes in the wool as they feed.

▲ Moth, Cottonball

RANGE: WARM REGIONS IN THE AMERICAS

HABITAT: COTTON

Cottonball moths are night-flying moths with two eye flashes on their wings. Their yellow-green caterpillars feed on cotton plants and can do tremendous damage to cotton crops.

▲ Moth, Geometrid

RANGE: SOUTHERN EURASIA, AFRICA

HABITAT: BROAD-LEAVED WOODS

Geometrid moths are unusual among moths in that they spread their wings flat when at rest. Their caterpillars, known as inchworms, form geometrical loops on leaves that can be damaging to the tree.

▼ Moth, Gypsy

RANGE: ORIGINALLY EURASIA, NOW ALSO N. AMERICA

HABITAT: TEMPERATE FORESTS

Gypsy moths were brought to North America in 1869 to provide silk. The project failed, the moths escaped, and in the wild their caterpillars do a great deal of damage, eating their way through both evergreen and broad-leaved forests. They can sometimes strip a whole forest in a single season.

▼ Moth, Hummingbird

RANGE: EURASIA EXCEPT SOUTH

HABITAT: SCRUB

Hummingbird moths can look remarkably like hummingbirds when they hover in front of flowers, sipping on nectar through their long feeding tube.

▼ Moth, Moon

RANGE: N. AMERICA

HABITAT: BROAD-LEAVED FORESTS

Like its African and Indian counterparts, the American moon moth is a large, beautiful, pale-colored moth with long, trailing tails on its wings. Its caterpillar feeds on trees, such as hickory, walnut, and birch.

▼ Moth, Oleander sphinx

RANGE: AFRICA, S. ASIA; SUMMER EUROPE

HABITAT: SUBTROPICAL FORESTS

The oleander sphinx or hawk moth is strikingly colored in green and purplish pink, but the patterns camouflage it very well against leaves. Its caterpillar feeds on oleander, periwinkle, and grapevine.

▲ Moth, Poplar sphinx

RANGE: EUROPE, W. ASIA

HABITAT: CATERPILLAR ON POPLAR TREES

Like other sphinx or hawk moths, the poplar feeds at night. During the day it rests on tree trunks, where its patterning keeps it remarkably well camouflaged against the bark.

▲ Moth, Tiger

RANGE: EURASIA, SOMETIMES N. AMERICA

HABITAT: WOODLAND, GARDENS

Tiger moths are so brightly colored that they look almost like butterflies. The colors warn predators that they taste nasty or mimic other nasty tasting species.

▲ Moth, White-lined sphinx

RANGE: N. AMERICA, EURASIA, AFRICA

HABITAT: WARM OPEN PLACES, INCLUDING DESERTS AND GARDENS

Like all sphinx or hawk moths, the white-lined is one of the fastest-flying insects and can reach speeds of more than 30 mph (50 km/h). It also flies long distances to breed.

▼ Plant bug

RANGE: WORLDWIDE

HABITAT: VEGETATED AREAS

Bugs are tiny insects that have needle-like mouth parts for piercing food and sucking out juices. Most plant bugs feed on leaves, including crops, but others feed on aphids.

▼ Pseudoscorpion

RANGE: WORLDWIDE, ESPECIALLY WARMER REGIONS

HABITAT: LEAF LITTER, TREE BARK

Pseudoscorpions are tiny relatives of the scorpion that live in leaf litter, but instead of stings in their tails they have venom glands in their pincers.

▼ Sawfly, Common

RANGE: WORLDWIDE, ESPECIALLY COOL N. HEMISPHERE

HABITAT: GARDENS, PASTURES, WOODS

Sawflies look a little like wasps, but do not have a sting. The female lays eggs on leaves, forming scars or galls.

▼ Scorpion

RANGE: WORLDWIDE, MOSTLY WARM PLACES

HABITAT: TYPICALLY DESERTS

Many scorpions have a dangerous sting in their tails, which can be fatal to humans. However, they usually catch their prey with their pincers.

▲ Scorpion, Whip

RANGE: TROPICAL N. AMERICA, S. AMERICA, S. ASIA

HABITAT: SOIL, CAVES, DESERTS

Whip scorpions have a long, thin tail and no sting. They are sometimes called vinegaroons because they can spray a vinegary liquid from the base of their tail when threatened.

▲ Scorpion, Wind

RANGE: C. AMERICA AND SOUTHERN N. AMERICA

HABITAT: WARM, DRY AREAS SUCH AS DESERTS

Wind scorpions, also known as sun spiders, are fast-running hunters that prey at night on insects and even small lizards.

▲ Scorpionfly, Common

RANGE: WORLDWIDE, MOSTLY N. HEMISPHERE

HABITAT: SHADY AREAS IN VEGETATION

Scorpionflies get their name because the male has swollen, upturned genitals in its tail that look just like a scorpion's sting.

▲ Silverfish

RANGE: WORLDWIDE, ESPECIALLY WARMER PLACES

HABITAT: DARK, WARM PLACES

Silverfish are tiny wingless insects. Some species live in dark, warm places indoors, eating flour, damp cloth, paper, and wallpaper paste.

▼ Skimmer

RANGE: WORLDWIDE

HABITAT: TYPICALLY NEAR SLOW-FLOWING STREAMS, PONDS

Skimmers are dragonflies with stout, flat bodies but often quite long wings, with a span up to 4 in (10 cm). They are usually seen flying near still or slow-moving water.

▼ Slug, Great black

RANGE: EUROPE, N. AMERICA

HABITAT: WOODLAND, FARMLAND, GARDENS

Slugs are mollusks, like snails, but have no shell and, as they move, lay down a trail of shiny mucus or slime to ease their passage. Slugs find the plants they eat by smell.

▼ Snail, Garden

RANGE: ORIGINALLY EUROPE, INTRODUCED ELSEWHERE

HABITAT: WOODLAND, FARMLAND, GARDENS

Snails are a kind of mollusk called gastropods, which feed on plants and animals using a special mouth part called a radula, filled with rows of teeth.

▼ Snakefly

RANGE: N. HEMISPHERE

HABITAT: WOODS, VEGETATION

Snakeflies get their name from their long necks, which they raise like a cobra to catch their prey, seizing it with a sudden lunge. They prey on beetle larvae and aphids.

▼ Spider, Black widow

RANGE: SOUTHERN U.S.A.

HABITAT: WOOD PILES OR GARBAGE

Female American black widows have a bite with venom more deadly than a rattlesnake. Although the amount of venom is small, it can kill a person unless anti-venom is given quickly.

▼ Spider, Common house

RANGE: EURASIA, N. AMERICA, AUSTRALIA

HABITAT: BUILDINGS

The house spider has long, hairy legs and builds large, flat webs in dark corners. It lurks in a silken tube under the web waiting for prey, then rushes out to catch any victim tangled in the sticky strands.

▲ Spider, Funnel web

RANGE: TROPICS WORLDWIDE EXCEPT S. AMERICA

HABITAT: ON THE GROUND, TREE TRUNKS

These spiders live in burrows and make funnel-shaped webs to trap their prey. The Sydney funnel-web is very poisonous.

▲ Spider, Crab

RANGE: WORLDWIDE

HABITAT: MEADOWS, GARDENS

Crab spiders get their name because they scuttle sideways like a crab. They do not make webs, although the smaller males use silk to tie the female down for mating. They usually lurk in wait for prey on flowers.

▲ Spider, Garden

RANGE: WORLDWIDE

HABITAT: GRASSLAND, FOREST, GARDENS

This spider weaves a web at night and waits during the day for prey to get caught in it. If the web is damaged, the spider eats it and makes a new one rather than repairing it.

▲ Spider, Golden-silk

RANGE: SUBTROPICAL, TROPICAL AMERICAS

HABITAT: DAMP OPEN FORESTS

These are spiders that build a strong web to protect them from predators and to capture prey. The drag line of their web is actually stronger than Kevlar, the fiber used in bullet-proof vests. Females weigh 100 times as much as males.

▲ Spider, Green lynx

RANGE: WORLDWIDE IN WARMER PLACES

HABITAT: SHRUBS, TALL GRASS

Lynx spiders are fast-moving hunters that rarely spin webs. Instead they chase their prey over plants, jumping from leaf to leaf. They have good eyesight and pounce on plant bugs, fire ants, and other insects, using their green color to hide them.

▲ Spider, Jumping

RANGE: WORLDWIDE, ESPECIALLY WARM REGIONS

HABITAT: WOODS, GRASS, GARDEN WALLS

Jumping spiders have unusually good eyesight for spiders and rely on jumping on victims to catch them rather than building a web. Before jumping, they attach a silk safety line to help them get back to their hideout.

▼ Spider, Lichen

RANGE: WARM REGIONS WORLDWIDE

HABITAT: ON THE GROUND, TREE TRUNKS

Spiders, such as the lichen, rely on their drab colors and soft outline to keep them hidden as they hunt at night. They can move sideways with enormous speed to catch prey.

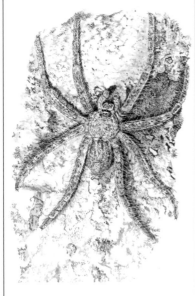

▼ Spider, Nursery-web

RANGE: WORLDWIDE

HABITAT: ON THE GROUND, WATER PLANTS

Nursery-web spiders weave webs not to catch prey but to protect their young. The female carries her egg sac with her until the eggs are almost ready to hatch, then spins a web around them. She then stands guard until they hatch.

▼ Spider, Ogre-faced

RANGE: WORLDWIDE

HABITAT: WOODLAND, GARDENS

The ogre-faced spider gets its name from its large-eyed face. It is a net-casting spider, which means it carries its web with it, and throws it like a net over its prey.

▼ Spider, Orchard

RANGE: WORLDWIDE

HABITAT: WOODLAND, GARDENS

The orchard spider is an orb-web spider, but does not spin a web. Instead, it sits on tree branches and waits to grab passing moths with its strong front legs, perhaps relying on its scent to attract them.

▼ Spider, Purse-web

RANGE: WORLDWIDE

HABITAT: IN THE GROUND

This spider weaves a long silk tube inside a sloping burrow. The top of the tube projects above the ground but is camouflaged with leaves. When an insect lands on the tube, the spider grabs it and drags it inside.

▼ Spider, Sheet web

RANGE: WORLDWIDE

HABITAT: GRASSLAND, FORESTS, GARDENS

This family of over 3,500 tiny spiders weaves sheetlike webs that hang from threads. Insects flying into these threads fall on to the web and are caught. Among many species are the money spiders and bowl-and-doilies.

▼ Spider, Spitting

RANGE: WARM REGIONS WORLDWIDE EXCEPT AUSTRALIA, NEW ZEALAND

HABITAT: UNDER ROCKS, IN BUILDINGS

This spider traps its prey by spitting out two zigzag lines of a sticky substance to literally stick the victim down.

▲ Spider, Trapdoor

RANGE: WORLDWIDE

HABITAT: IN THE GROUND

Trapdoor spiders live in burrows with hinged lids at the top. The spider waits in its burrow until it senses prey moving overhead, then jumps out of the door and grabs the prey.

▲ Spider, Water

RANGE: EURASIA

HABITAT: SLOW FLOWING OR STILL WATER

This is the only spider to spend its life underwater. It can swim and dive and is able to live in the water by spinning itself a bell-shaped air bubble from which it can launch its attacks on prey.

▲ Spider, Wolf

RANGE: WORLDWIDE

HABITAT: VARIED

Wolf spiders are roving hunters with sharp eyesight that creep up on prey and seize it after a final dash. Females weave silk cocoons for their eggs.

▲ Stick insect

RANGE: WORLDWIDE, ESPECIALLY AUSTRALASIA

HABITAT: ON SHRUBS AND TREES

Stick insects look so much like twigs that, when they are motionless during the day, predatory birds can hardly see them. They move to feed on leaves at night.

▼ Stinkbug

RANGE: WORLDWIDE

HABITAT: SHRUBS AND TREES

Stinkbugs get their name from the foul-smelling liquid that they squirt at any attacker. Like all bugs they suck nourishment from plants or insects.

▼ Stonefly, Common

RANGE: WORLDWIDE EXCEPT AUSTRALIA

HABITAT: PLANTS NEAR STREAMS

Stoneflies look a little like dragonflies, but they are not strong fliers and spend much of the day resting on stones with their wings folded. They also feed mostly on plants, though some hunt insects.

▼ Sweetheart underwing

RANGE: N. AMERICA

HABITAT: FOREST, GARDENS

This moth is usually very hard to see because its mottled colors blend so well into the bark of the tree where it rests during the day, but if alarmed it flashes the bright pink underwings that give it its name to startle the attacker.

▲ Tarantula, Red-kneed

RANGE: WARM REGIONS WORLDWIDE, ESPECIALLY S. AMERICA

HABITAT: DESERT, FOREST

Tarantulas are big spiders. The largest are called bird-eating spiders because they sometimes prey on small birds. These can measure up to 11 in (28 cm) across.

▲ Termite, Drywood

RANGE: TROPICS

HABITAT: DRY WOOD, INCLUDING TIMBER

These termites attack dry wood, including furniture, beams, and planks in houses. Microorganisms in their gut help them to digest the wood. Special soldier termites with large heads and horns defend the colony.

▲ Termite, Snouted

RANGE: TROPICS

HABITAT: ON THE GROUND

Most termite colonies have special soldiers to defend them against enemies, such as ants. The snouted termite soldiers have especially long snouts, which they use to spray a sticky, foul-smelling fluid at any unfortunate intruder.

▼ Termite, Subterranean

RANGE: TROPICS

HABITAT: IN SOIL AND WOOD

These termites live in underground nests in warm, wooded areas. They feed on the wood of rotting trees and their roots, but some species are also serious timber pests.

▼ Tick, Hard

RANGE: WORLDWIDE

HABITAT: ON BIRD, MAMMAL, REPTILE HOSTS

Ticks are parasites that feed on the blood of birds, mammals, and reptiles. Young ticks stick on their host for several days while feeding, then drop off to turn into an adult.

▼ Treehopper

RANGE: WARMER REGIONS WORLDWIDE

HABITAT: ON TREES

These little bugs are sometimes known as thorn bugs because they have an extraordinary thorn-shaped extension on their thorax called a pronotun. This acts as a disguise and also makes them difficult to eat.

▼ Wasp, Blue-black spider

RANGE: WORLDWIDE, ESPECIALLY WARMER REGIONS

HABITAT: VARIED, NEAR SPIDERS

Adult spider wasps feed on nectar, but when they are about to lay their eggs, the female will catch spiders by paralyzing them with her sting. She then drags the spider to her nest, lays an egg, and seals it. The spider will provide food for the hatchling.

▲ Wasp, Common

RANGE: EURASIA

HABITAT: ATTICS OR BURROWS

These wasps build paper nests in attics or in the ground. They feed on nectar and ripe fruit, but also catch insects to feed their young. Such wasps are well known for the sting at the end of their tail.

▲ Wasp, Gall

RANGE: WORLDWIDE, MOSTLY N. HEMISPHERE

HABITAT: HOST TREES, PLANTS

Gall wasps are tiny wasps that lay their eggs on plants. The plant then produces a scar called a gall, which protects and nourishes the larvae as they hatch.

▲ Wasp, Ichneumon

RANGE: WORLDWIDE, ESPECIALLY TEMPERATE REGIONS

HABITAT: HOST INSECTS SUCH AS BEETLES

These wasps lay their eggs on or inside other insects or their larvae. When the eggs hatch the larvae feed on the host.

▼ Wasp, Paper

RANGE: WORLDWIDE

HABITAT: VARIED

Paper wasps belong to the family of social wasps that live in colonies organized around a queen. They build nests of papery material made from chewed wood and saliva.

▼ Weevil, Boll

RANGE: SOUTHERN U.S.A.

HABITAT: COTTONFIELDS

Weevils are beetle-like insects that eat plants. The boll weevil attacks the bolls (seed pods) of cotton plants and can devastate a cotton crop. The female can lay an egg in up to 300 bolls.

▼ Woodlouse

RANGE: EURASIA

HABITAT: LEAF LITTER, WOOD DEBRIS

Woodlice are crustaceans like crabs, but live on land. They hide in moist, dark places in the day and come out at night to feed on decaying plant matter and insect corpses.

▼ Yellow jacket

RANGE: N. AMERICA

HABITAT: FOREST, FIELDS, TOWNS

Yellow jackets are the American equivalents of European wasps. Like them, they feed on nectar and other sweet things, but prey on insects to feed their young. The female stings aggressively if her nest is threatened.

Glossary

aestivation A time of dormancy in hot or dry weather. Many animals in the warm subtropics aestivate during the long dry season.

algae Plantlike organisms that usually live in water. Most are microscopic, but some seaweeds can be many meters long.

amphibian A creature that begins its life as an egg in water but spends much of its adult life on land.

arboreal Dwelling mainly in (forest) trees.

arthropods The largest group of invertebrate animals, including insects, spiders, and crustaceans.

biome A large, characteristic grouping of plants and animals adapted to survive in a particular geographic zone.

camouflage Colors or patterns on an animal that make it difficult to see against its background. *See also* mimicry.

carnivore An animal that eats meat. More particularly, carnivores are mammals belonging to the order Carnivora.

carrion The remains of recently dead animals, fed upon by meat-eaters, such as vultures.

cells Microscopically small packages from which all living things are made up.

class Level in the system of animal classification below a phylum. Amphibians are one class; reptiles are another.

cold-blooded See ectothermic.

colony Large group of animals of the same species living together.

deciduous Tree that loses its leaves in fall to save water during the winter.

diurnal Active during the day, or occurring daily.

dormancy A sleeplike state in which a plant or animal ceases to be active. *See also* aestivation, hibernation.

echolocation A way in which animals, such as bats and whales, find their way around, or find prey by sending out bursts of sounds and detecting the reflections.

ectothermic Animal with a body temperature that depends mainly on its surroundings, like reptiles. Also known as cold-blooded.

endemic Species native to an area.

endothermic Animal that is able to maintain its own constant body temperature, like mammals. Also known as warm-blooded.

epiphyte Plant that grows in trees, high off the ground.

evolution Gradual changing of animal species through time; usually explained by Darwin's theory of natural selection.

exoskeleton A skeleton forming a hard shell around the outside of its body, like an insect's.

extinction The final disappearance of a species.

family A level in the system of animal classification below an order. Families, such as big cats and eagles, are divided into genera.

food chain A who-eats-who line, linking living species in which each species eats the next in the chain.

food web An interlinking network of food chains from a particular environment. Typically, each species in the web is involved in more than one food chain.

genus (plural **genera**) A level in the system of animal classification below a family. Genera are divided into species.

grub Young insect larva with a thick, soft body which may or may not have legs.

habitat The natural surroundings an animal needs to survive.

herbivore Animal that feeds mainly on plants.

hibernation Deep, sleeplike period of dormancy in winter during which an animal's body cools and its body processes slow down.

host Animal used by a parasite for its food and home.

incubation The process whereby an embryo develops inside an egg before hatching.

insectivore Animal that eats mainly insects.

invertebrate Any animal that does not have a backbone, such as insects and crustaceans.

kingdom One of the five basic divisions of the living world, such as animals or plants.

larva (plural **larvae**) A young animal, such as an insect, that looks completely different from its adult form. *See also* pupa.

lepidoptera The order of insects made up by the 150,000 species of butterfly and moth.

life-cycle All the stages in the life of an animal, from its beginning through reproduction to its death.

marsupial A mammal in which babies finish developing in a pouch, not inside the mother's womb.

metamorphosis The dramatic change in body shape as a young animal becomes an adult, such as when a tadpole becomes a frog or a caterpillar becomes a butterfly.

migration Long journey made, often yearly, by animals to breed or find food. Most animals that migrate leave at particular times and follow particular routes, guided by instinct.

mimicry A kind of camouflage in which an animal looks like another animal, plant, or object. Many insects are mimics.

niche The place or role in a habitat which an animal can fill.

nocturnal Active at night.

nymph Young insect resembling its parents, but without fully formed reproductive organs and often a very different way of life.

order Level in the system of animal classification below class. Orders, such as all the primates, are divided into families.

Orthoptera Order of 18,000 insects species, mostly with long back legs for jumping, including grasshoppers, crickets, and locusts.

parasite An animal that lives or feeds on or inside another living animal. Most parasites are tiny and only weaken their host animal.

photosynthesis The processes that allow plants to capture energy from the sun and store it as sugars.

phylum (plural **phyla**). Level in the system of animal classification below kingdom. Phyla are divided into classes.

plankton Microscopic organisms that float in lakes and oceans. Plankton include algae.

prairie Grassland found in North America, or any area of tall grass in temperate regions.

predator Animal that kills other animals and eats them.

prehensile Able to curl around things and grip them.

proboscis A nose or long noselike set of mouthparts. An elephant's trunk is a proboscis; so is a butterfly's nectar-sipping tongue.

pupa (plural **pupae**) Stage in the life cycle of an insect in which the larva's body breaks down and is rebuilt as an adult. Pupae usually have a hard outer case, often inside a cocoon.

savanna Dry, tropical grassland, especially in Africa.

scavenger Animal that lives on leftovers, including human refuse and remains of predator's kills.

species A single kind of living thing. Members of a species can breed with each other, producing offspring like themselves.

steppe Grassland in Eastern Europe and Asia, or any area of short grass in temperate regions.

temperate Zone with moderate temperatures—basically the areas of the world between the tropics and the polar regions.

terrestrial Living mainly on the ground.

territory Area claimed by an animal, either for feeding or breeding.

understory Layer of vegetation on the ground in forests.

vertebrate Animal with a backbone—basically fish, mammals, reptiles, amphibians, and birds.

warm-blooded See endothermic.

Acknowledgments

PHOTOGRAPHIC CREDITS

t = top; b = bottom; c = center; l = left; r = right
OSF = Oxford Scientific Films; BBC NHU = BBC Natural History Unit; FLPA = Frank Lane Picture Agency

2t Manoj Shah/gettyOneStone, **2c** Chase Swift/CORBIS, **2b** Eyal Bartov/OSF; **3tl** Terry Heathcote/OSF, **3tr** David Tipling/BBC NHU, **3cl** Tom Ulrich/OSF, **3cr** Galen Rowell/CORBIS, **3b** Kennan Ward/CORBIS; **4/5** Digital Vision; **6&7** Manoj Shah/gettyOneStone; **7t** Richard Du Toit/BBC NHU, **7b** Paul Franklin/OSF; **11t** Ross Couper-Johnston/BBC NHU, **11c** Martha Holmes/BBC NHU, **11bl** Wendy Shatti & Bob Rozinski/OSF; **17t** Michael Powles/OSF, **17c** Keith Scholey/BBC NHU, **17bl** Fritz Polking/FLPA/CORBIS, **17br** Bruce Davidson/BBC NHU; **21t** Hans & Judy Beste/OSF, **21c** A.G.(Bert) Wells/OSF, **21bl** John Cancalosi/BBC NHU, **21br** Robin Bush/OSF; **22/23** Chase Swift/CORBIS, **23t** J.A.L.Cooke/OSF, **23b** Richard Davies/OSF; **27t** Anup Shah/BBC NHU, **27c** Dieter Plage/OSF, **27bl** Lynn Stone/BBC NHU, **27br** Ardea; **33t** Neil P. Lucas/BBC NHU, **33c** Ingo Arndt/BBC NHU, **33bl** Michael Fogden/OSF, **33br** Morley Read/BBC NHU; **36** Anup Shah/BBC NHU; **37t** Tom Brakefield/CORBIS, **37c** Anup Shah/BBC NHU, **37b** CORBIS; **38/39** Eyal Bartov/OSF, **39t** Gallow Images/CORBIS, **39b** Michael Fogden/OSF; **43t** Rob Nummington/OSF, **43c** Joe MacDonald/CORBIS, **43bl** Tony Heald/BBC NHU, **43br** Francois Merlet FLPA; **49tl** Christoph Becker/BBC NHU, **49tr** Daniel J Cox/OSF, **49c** Paul N. Johnson/BBC NHU, **49b** Eyal Bartov/OSF; **53t** J.A.L. Cooke/OSF, **53c** Marty Stouffer/Animals Animals/OSF, **53b** Andrew Watson/Travel Ink; **54/55** Terry Heathcote/OSF; **55t** Niall Benvie/BBC NHU, **55b** Terry Heathcote/OSF; **58** Jim Hallett/BBC NHU; **59t** Staffan Windstrand/BBC NHU, **59c** Konrad Wothe/OSF, **59b** Mark Yates/BBC NHU; **65t** Jose Schell/BBC NHU, **65c** David Welling/BBC NHU, **65b** Tom Lazar/BBC NHU; **68** Stanley Breeden/OSF; **69t** Lynn Stone/BBC NHU, **69c** Michael Powles/OSF, **69b** www.savechinastigers.org; **73t** Robin Bush/OSF, **73c** FLPA/CORBIS, **73bl** Steve Turner/OSF, **73br** Doug Wechsler/OSF; **74/75** Tom Ulrich/OSF, **75t** Vladimir Kolbintsev/BBC NHU, **75b** Ernest Wilkinson/OSF; **79t** Jeff Vanuga/CORBIS, **79b** Jack Wilburn/Animals Animals/OSF; **84** G.&H. Denzau/BBC NHU; **85t** Carlos Sanchez/OSF, **85b** Michael Powles/OSF; **86/87** Kennan Ward/CORBIS, **87t** Richard Packwood/OSF, **87b** Andrey Zvoznikov/BBC NHU; **90** Peter Weimann/Animals Animals/OSF; **91t** Christoph Becker/BBC NHU, **91b** Papilio/CORBIS; **97t** David M. Dennis/OSF, **97b** Tom Vezo/BBC NHU; **98/99** David Tipling/BBC NHU; **99t** ECOSCENE/Hulme, **99c** Frithjof Skibbe/OSF, **99b** Chris Gomersall/BBC NHU; **103t** Jeff Foott/BBC NHU, **103b** Daniel J Cox/OSF; **109t** Arnoud van den Berg, **109b** Keith Ringland/OSF; **113t** Bruce Davidson/BBC NHU, **113b** Liz & Tony Bomford/OSF; **115t** Martyn Colbeck/OSF, **115c** David Muench/CORBIS, **115b** Richard Packwood/OSF; **114/115** Galen Rowell/CORBIS

ARTWORK CREDITS

10–11, 86–87, 98–99 Gill Tomblin
12–13, 28–29, 44–45, 92–93, 104–5, 118–19 Russell Barnett
16–17, 36–37 Richard Bonson
20–21, 32–33, 68–69, 72–73, 78–79, 84–85 Michael Woods
26–27, 52–53, 64–65 Chris Orr Associates
42–43 Christian Webb/Temple Rogers
48–49, 108–9, 112–13 Peter David Scott/ Wildlife Art Agency
58–59, 90–91 Brian Delf
60–61, 80–81, 96–97, 102–3, 114–15 Ian Jackson/Wildlife Art Agency

Maps
Alan Collinson Design

Mammals
Graham Allen, Sandra Doyle/Wildlife Art Agency, John Francis, Tudor Humphries, Eric Robson, Dick Twinney, Michael Woods

Birds
Norman Arlott, Dianne Breeze, Chris Christoforou, Barry Croucher/Wildlife Art Agency, Malcolm Ellis, Robert Gilmour, Peter Hayman, Denys Ovenden, David Quinn, Chris Rose, Andrew Robinson, Owen Williams, Ken Wood, Michael Woods

Reptiles
Steve Kirk, Alan Male, Eric Robson, Peter David Scott/Wildlife Art Agency

Amphibians
Robin Boutell/ Wildlife Art Agency, Alan Male

Insects and Invertebrates
Joanne Cowne, Sandra Doyle/ Wildlife Art Agency, Ian Jackson/Wildlife Art Agency, Bridget James, Steve Kirk, Adrian Lascom, Alan Male, Colin Newman, Steve Roberts, Michael Woods

Fish
Colin Newman

Every effort has been made to credit all photographs and illustrations correctly. Marshall Editions apologizes for any unintentional omissions or errors and, if informed of any such cases, would be pleased to update any future editions.